SHROPSHIRE FROM THE AIR

MAN AND THE LANDSCAPE

Michael Watson and Chris Musson

Shropshire
Books

Front cover: Stitt Hill, Ratlinghope

Title Page: Camp Ring, Culmington

Back Cover: Rushbury

© Michael Watson and Chris Musson 1993
   Reprinted 1994

ISBN: 0-903802-57-0

Cover and book design: Paul Brasenell

Editing: Helen Sample

Published by Shropshire Books,
the Publishing Division of the Leisure Services Department
of Shropshire County Council.

Printed by Precision Colour Printing, Telford

ACKNOWLEDGMENTS

Thanks are due to the Cambridge University Committee for Aerial Photography for permission to reproduce photographs 16, 42, 46, 47 and 53 (Cambridge University Collection of Air Photographs: Copyright Reserved). Photographs 11 and 39 are © Crown Copyright 1993 and are reproduced with the permission of the Controller of HMSO.

All the other photographs used in this book are from collections of the Clwyd-Powys Archaeological Trust (Copyright Reserved), and are reproduced here with their kind permission. The authors would like to take this opportunity to thank the staffs of both Clwyd-Powys Archaeological Trust and the Royal Commission on the Historical Monuments of England for their work in facilitating much of the aerial archaeology carried out in Shropshire since the 1970s.

Finally, grateful thanks must also be extended to Brenda Gill for her sterling efforts in producing the typescript.

CONTENTS

ABOUT THE AUTHORS

Michael Watson was born and grew up in Sheffield where his archaeological interests were first developed. He read archaeology at University College Cardiff, and, after a period of postgraduate research, came to Shropshire in 1980 as an Archaeological Officer for the County Council. Since then he has been closely involved in the aerial archaeology of Shropshire. He is currently the Head of Archaeology for the Leisure Services Department of Shropshire County Council.

Chris Musson originally trained and practised as an architect. In the early 1970s, however, he switched careers to become one of Britain's first full-time archaeological excavators with the Rescue Archaeology Group. His first venture into the air, in 1974, took place from Sleap Airport, in Shropshire, and his fascination with the landscape and aerial archaeology of the county has continued ever since. In 1986 he became the first Investigator in Air Photography with the Royal Commission on the Ancient and Historical Monuments of Wales, but still finds time each year to record the impact of man on the landscape on the 'wrong' side of Offa's Dyke.

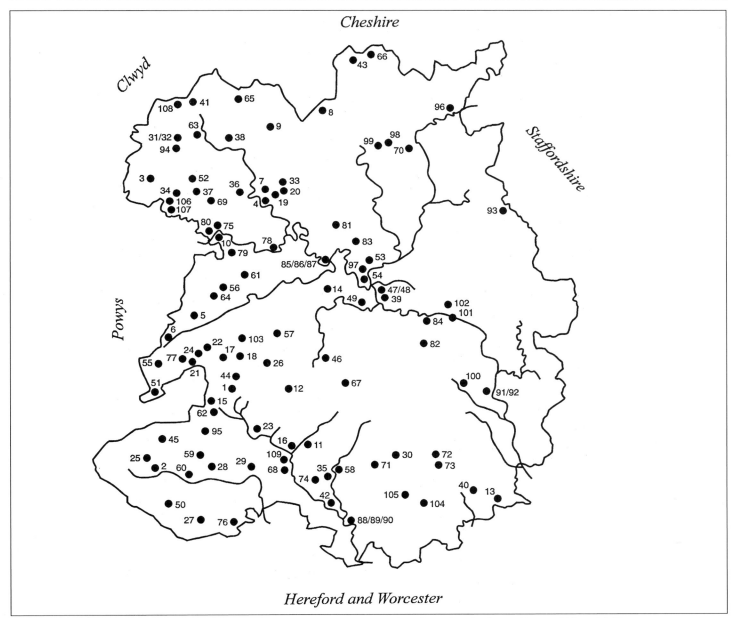

The numbers on this map refer to individual photographs. See also the list on Pages 116 and 117.

Buildwas Power Station and Ironbridge

INTRODUCTION

Shropshire is justly famed for the beauty and diversity of its landscape and scenery. Over millions of years natural forces have created a richly varied canvas of landforms on to which man has etched his indelible mark. Indeed, the Shropshire landscape that we see today is almost entirely the product of man's influence over the last six thousand years. It is a vibrant, living testimony to millenia of human endeavour and to the succession of peoples who have lived, worked, worshipped and died in the area we know today as Shropshire. Increasingly people are becoming more aware of the county's historic landscapes and more involved in recognising and interpreting their constituent parts. Few however, have the opportunity to appreciate and enjoy these landscapes from the air, though this book aims to let them do so at second hand. Our hope is that the reader will gain new and perhaps surprising insights into Shropshire's past, while at the same time enjoying the striking beauty of its historical sites and ancient monuments. The book does not set out to tell the full story of the county's archaeological and historical development; for local people and visitors alike, however, it should give some idea of the rich heritage that goes to make up the Shropshire that we know today.

The photographs, mostly taken by Chris Musson between 1979 and 1993, have been chosen to illustrate those aspects of Shropshire's past which we consider of particular importance and which have made a significant impact on the evolution of the landscape. Inevitably when dealing with the largest inland county in England and one so rich in archaeological sites and monuments, the choice of photographs must be very selective. Those presented here are only a tiny proportion of the ten thousand or so aerial views accumulated over the past fifteen years through locally-based reconnaissance. We believe, however, that they illustrate effectively the major elements and themes of Shropshire's historic and prehistoric past.

The book begins with a series of representative landscape views that form the context for the county's surviving historic remains. These are followed by photographs of specific archaeological sites and historic landscapes, each accompanied by a short interpretative and descriptive text by Michael Watson. These are arranged in broadly chronological sequence, but it will soon become apparent that few individual sites or landscapes exist in chronological isolation; instead, each forms part of a complex 'over-printing' or palimpsest of successive periods, in the progressively more complex landscape that we recognise today.

AERIAL PHOTOGRAPHY AND AERIAL ARCHAEOLOGY

It will be useful here to outline briefly the principal techniques of aerial archaeology employed, to permit a better understanding of the photographs themselves. The advent of aerial survey has been one of the greatest developments in twentieth-century archaeology. Its impact has fundamentally altered many of our ideas about the past, in particular the nature and development of early settlement in Britain. This remarkable achievement is due to the power of aerial photography to reveal previously unsuspected sites and to improve understanding of known ones. The aerial view also allows individual sites and monuments to be viewed in their broader setting and in relation to other sites and relict landscape features. Townscapes, village plans and general settlement patterns are further aspects of the historic environment that can benefit greatly through study from the air.

From the air historic features reveal themselves in three main forms: shadowmarks, soilmarks and cropmarks. Shadowmarks are produced by those man-made features or earthworks which survive in an upstanding form in the landscape. If viewed from the air when the sun is low in the sky, in the early morning or late evening or at any time of good weather in winter, these often meagre earthworks are considerably enhanced by the shadows cast. Slight features, almost invisible on the ground, can be thrown into strikingly clear relief. Photograph 1 shows a shadowmark site that was discovered from the air. Its low earthworks, whose date and function remain unknown, are situated on the south side of Linley Hill, near Bishops Castle. The photograph was taken early one winter morning when the shadows and highlights cast by the low sun picked out the earthworks to maximum effect. Light snowfall can also accentuate slight earthworks, as seen in Photograph 2. Here a prehistoric enclosure known as Castle Idris, near Newcastle-on-Clun, is picked out by the differential drifting and melting of snow around its encircling rampart - see Photograph 77 (Vyrnwy fields) for another snow scene in a broader landscape context.

Soilmark sites are formed when buried archaeological features are ploughed, the discolouration of the newly disturbed soil permitting their discovery and recording. Few soilmark sites have yet been located in Shropshire, though Photograph 3 shows a striking example in the form of an oval enclosure at Bwlch Farm, near Oswestry, seen shortly after ploughing. The former defensive banks are visible as lighter bands of soil, in contrast to the darker material of the surrounding and now filled-in ditch. Modern field drains partially cutting through the enclosure also show as soilmarks.

In many ways the power of aerial archaeology is best illustrated in the so-called cropmark site. Cropmarks are produced by the effect of buried archaeological features on the growth of crops above them (see Figure. 1). Thus, buried ditches will present crops with a deeper, richer and moister soil rooting medium than the surrounding soil. This will cause the crop above the ditch to grow richer and taller, and to stay green longer as it ripens more slowly than the surrounding plants. Conversely, a crop growing above a buried wall or gravel road-surface will have access to less nutrition and moisture and so will be stunted in growth and will ripen sooner. These effects are particularly emphasised in times of drought. The resulting differences of colour in arable fields becomes startlingly clear when seen from the air, permitting the recording of archaeological remains which are wholly or mainly invisible from the ground. In Photograph 4, the buried ditch of a curvilinear enclosure (near Adcote, north Shropshire) stands out starkly as a band of darker growth against the lighter (riper) crop in the rest of the field. On occasions the extra height of crops above buried features can enable sites to be revealed as shadowmarks, as for example in the ditched enclosure at Rowley, near Worthen illustrated in Photograph 5. In Britain it is usually the deep-rooted cereal crops, such as barley and oats, that produce the best cropmarks, though oil-seed rape, peas and root-crops of

Photo 1

Photo 2

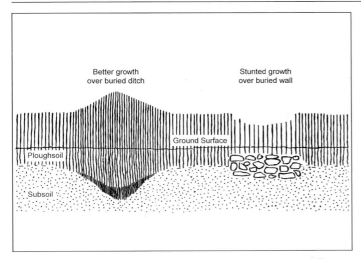

Better growth over buried ditch

Stunted growth over buried wall

Ground Surface

Ploughsoil

Subsoil

Figure 1

Photo 4

Photo 3

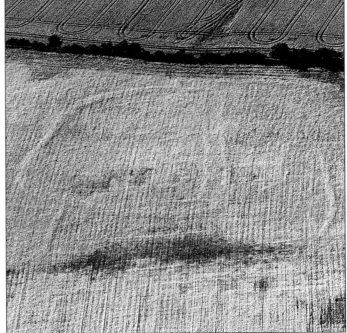

Photo 5

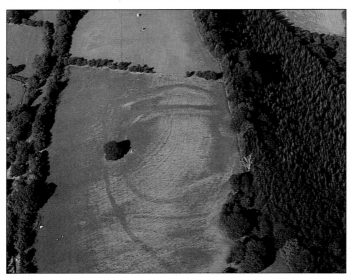

Photo 6

various kinds can be equally responsive in some circumstances. Occasionally, though, in conditions of severe drought, even grass can produce cropmarks. Photograph 6 shows an example on a pasture hilltop at Stocktonwood, near Chirbury, where severe parching has dramatically outlined the filled-in ditches of an almost levelled pre-Roman hillfort.

But it is not just deeply buried remains that manifest themselves as cropmarks, as is shown by the remarkable pattern recorded in Photograph 7. The house to the left is Boreatton Hall, near Baschurch, a country residence built about 1700. During the long, dry summer of 1990 geometric cropmarks in the arable field to the right of the Hall revealed a previously unrecorded large formal garden, with its rectangular flower-beds, paths and walkways. The garden was probably laid out at the time the Hall was built and thus not only serves to set the Hall within its contemporary landscape, but also sheds new light on the status and social aspirations of its creators. In itself this is a fitting tribute to the impact, importance and effectiveness of aerial archaeology in drawing back the shutters of the past, in Shropshire as in other parts of Britain.

Photo 7

Photo 8

WHIXALL MOSS

The great raised mire of Whixall Moss straddles the England-Wales border seven kilometres east of Ellesmere. Together with Fenn's Moss, it covers an area of some 646 hectares and is the most extensive lowland peat bog in England. The Moss was formerly a glacial mere that gradually silted up during the warmer climate following the last retreat of the ice, around ten thousand years ago, and eventually became a peat bog. These peat resources have been exploited for centuries, until large-scale commercial extraction ceased in 1991. The extent of the peat extraction is marked by row after row of narrow linear cuttings. These are bounded on the right by the straight course of the Llangollen Canal, opened here in 1805, though not before major engineering problems had been overcome in crossing the Moss. Parliamentary enclosure of Whixall Moss during the eighteenth and nineteenth centuries greatly reduced its size; in this view the surrounding regular fields reflect this process of enclosure. In recent years, however, some of these enclosures have begun to revert to fenland; the encroachment of scrub and tree cover is particularly noticeable to the right of the canal.

Photo 9

THE NORTH SHROPSHIRE LAKES

The lakes and meres around the north Shropshire town of Ellesmere create one of the most distinctive of the county's many varied landscapes. There are seven lakes in total, and the area is justly known as the 'Shropshire Lake District'. This view, looking north, shows four of the meres, with White Mere in the foreground, and beyond from left to right Blake Mere, Newton Mere and Cole Mere. Each of these little lakes is a legacy of the last Ice Age, when large blocks of ice left behind by the retreating glaciers became buried by glacial debris. In time the buried ice melted, to leave behind hollows which in turn became water-filled lakes. Together the meres make one of the finest areas of wetland habitat to be found in Britain, with a richly diverse pattern of flora and fauna. They also attract thousands of visitors each year, for the boating and fishing which they provide, and for the distinctive character of the landscape.

Photo 10

THE RIVER SEVERN

The River Severn is perhaps the best known and best loved of all Shropshire's natural landscape features. From earliest times it has served variously as an inland waterway, boundary, fishery, water supply and leisure facility. Towns such as Bridgnorth and Shrewsbury owe their origins to the defensive and strategic potential of the river. The Severn has, therefore, made a major contribution to the prosperity and development of the county.   After descending from the Welsh Hills the Severn enters the lowland Shropshire plain near Melverley, in a series of wide meandering loops; this view shows its confluence with the River Vyrnwy, visible in the middle distance to the left of the Severn. From Melverley the Severn flows eastward along its own broad flood-plain in the direction of the Wrekin, (on the horizon at top right), before flowing through the narrow gap of the Ironbridge Gorge. Until the last glaciation the Severn probably flowed northwards to the Dee Estuary, but when this route was blocked by the ice sheets of twenty thousand to thirteen thousand years ago a series of lakes was created, which eventually overflowed eastward to cut the Ironbridge Gorge. The last Ice Age thus brought the county one of its greatest natural resources, throughout prehistory and onwards to the present day.

Photo 11

WENLOCK EDGE

Wenlock Edge running unbroken for some twenty-five kilometres between Ironbridge and Craven Arms is perhaps the finest geological escarpment in Britain. It is formed of a thick band of limestone, laid down four hundred and twenty million years ago under a shallow tropical sea. This view looks north-east along the Edge from its southern end near Strefford. The steep wooded west-facing scarp overlooks Apedale to the left, with the meandering course of the Lake Brook at its foot. To the right the gentle dip-slope leads to a second and higher limestone escarpment running parallel to the first, with the valley of Hope Dale between. During the Middle Ages much of Wenlock Edge lay within the royal preserve of Long Forest, so named from its length, extending as it did along the full extent of Wenlock Edge. Economically, however, the Edge has always been most heavily exploited for its native limestone. Since at least the Middle Ages this has been extensively used as a building material, for instance at Wenlock Priory (Photograph 84). Other uses of the stone have been for agricultural lime, cement, smelting flux in iron-making, and for roadstone in more recent times. The remains of this limestone industry survive along many parts of the Edge, and near Much Wenlock itself there are working quarries still.

Photo 12

WYRE FOREST

In the south-east tip of the county, between Cleobury Mortimer and the River Severn, lies the extensive tract of woodland known as the Wyre Forest. This view looks northward from a point on the county boundary with Worcestershire, which here follows the valley of the Dowles Brook in the foreground. The Forest was formerly more extensive but piecemeal colonisation from the medieval period onwards has reduced it to its present size. In the earlier Middle Ages it was a royal hunting forest but despite this from the twelfth century onwards isolated farms were being carved out of it. The long wedge of farmland in the middle distance is the result of this medieval colonisation and clearance. By the eighteenth century the Wyre Forest had become an important source of timber for industry, particularly for the production of charcoal. As a result much of the Forest was coppiced; the remnants of these strictly managed coppices are still much in evidence. More recently, large areas of the Forest have been replanted by the Foresty Commission in formal regulated plantations, though there are still attractive walks through various parts of the woodland.

Photo 13

THE LONG MYND

The landscape of the south Shropshire hills is in many ways epitomised by the towering mass of the Long Mynd. This bleak, featureless plateau comprises some of the oldest rocks in Britain, Precambrian sandstones laid down under a shallow sea some six to five hundred million years ago. More recently, during the last Ice Age, the meltwaters from the great ice sheets to the north and west cut a series of deep narrow valleys, known as 'batches', across the eastern slopes of the plateau. These give the Mynd its distinctive serrated appearance, as in this view looking south.

Settlement is confined to the surrounding valley bottoms, and only on the Long Mynd's lower slopes have fields been carved out to create areas of improved pasture. In the foreground can be seen the greens and bunkers of Church Stretton golf course, together with the small hillfort of Bodbury Ring, (centre), sited on a promontory overlooking the Cardingmill Valley. In the further distance the heather and bracken-covered plateau is today largely the preserve of the sheep and the more intrepid of the hiking fraternity.

MAMMOTHS AT NORTON FARM QUARRY, CONDOVER

The sand and gravel quarry at Norton Farm, Condover, in the background of this photograph, is located four kilometres south of Shrewsbury. Here, one September morning in 1986, Mrs Eve Roberts, while walking her dog, noticed some unusually large bones on the top of a spoil-heap. The bones had been encountered earlier that morning during the mechanical stripping of the overburden in a newly extended portion of the quarry. On examination the bones proved to be those of a prehistoric mammoth. Subsequent excavations recovered in total the remains of four mammoths, one adult male and three infants - a remarkable find. The find-spot was within a natural hollow, the remnant of a glacial pond which had become an open, but treacherous, pool by the time the mammoths wandered into it and met their deaths. Shomere Pool, in the foreground, is another glacial pool that has survived to the present day, like Bomere Pool, above and to the right.

Radiocarbon dating of the bones showed that the adult mammoth had lived about twelve thousand seven hundred years ago, thus demonstrating that mammoths had survived in Britain until the final stages of the last Ice Age, much later than previously assumed. The remains included the most complete adult mammoth skeleton ever found in Britain and one of the finest in western Europe. No evidence was found for any human involvement in the deaths of the Condover mammoths, but early hunter-gatherers are likely to have been active in the region during this period, perhaps eventually hunting to extinction the last of the Shropshire mammoths.

Photo 14

13

Photo 15

THE ROVERIES, LYDHAM

The arrival of the first agriculturalists probably some time during the fourth millenium BC has left few recognisable traces in the present-day landscape of Shropshire. That early agricultural communities, the so-called 'Neolithic' or New Stone Age farmers, were active in Shropshire is amply demonstrated, however, by frequent finds of their stone tools and implements. One place where traces of their activity have been encountered more directly is on the summit of the hill known as The Roveries, just north of Lydham, in south-west Shropshire. The Roveries is a prominent dome-shaped hill at the head of the Camlad Valley. Its natural defensive qualities led to its use during the later prehistoric

period for a hillfort, enclosing just over two hectares within a massive stone-faced rampart. A much earlier phase of occupation came to light in 1960 when excavations in the centre of the hillfort located a hearth which was associated with Neolithic pottery. Further Neolithic potsherds were found beneath the rampart near the northern entrance, showing that the hill had been occupied two thousand years or more before a later community erected the Iron Age defences of the hillfort. The Roveries, commanding the Camlad-Onny gap and the Lydham pass to the south-west of the Long Mynd, would have offered an attractive settlement site for early Neolithic colonists and Iron Age communities alike.

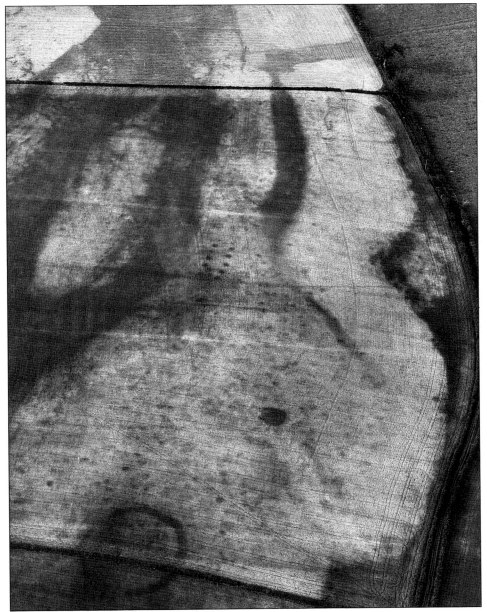

Photo 16

PREHISTORIC RITUAL SITES AT STREFFORD

At Strefford, four kilometres north of Craven Arms, air photography has revealed a series of cropmarks that may be those of a ritual and funerary complex of late Neolithic/Early Bronze Age date (circa 2500 - 2000 BC) .

Sited on the edge of a gravel terrace, overlooking the Quinny Brook, is a circular cropmark enclosure, seen at bottom left in this Cambridge University photograph. It is some sixty metres in diameter and has three gaps or entrances through a wide and substantial ditch. It bears some resemblance to the ritual 'henge monuments' that are so characteristic of the third millenium BC, but which have so far eluded detection in Shropshire. Some one hundred metres north of the circle can be seen two parallel lines of pits about ten metres apart, visible as five pairs of dots at the centre of the photograph. These seem to be aligned on the 'henge' enclosure and may be associated and contemporary with it. The pits probably held upright timbers, perhaps forming a ceremonial avenue leading to the henge - an arrangement noted at similar sites elsewhere in the country.

In the immediate vicinity, though not visible in this photograph, are a number of other circular cropmarks, or 'ring-ditches', most likely the remains of round barrows of early Bronze Age date (see also Photographs 19 and 20). These ring-ditches give further support to the idea of this locality as an important ritual and funerary centre in the early prehistoric period, between four and five thousand years ago.

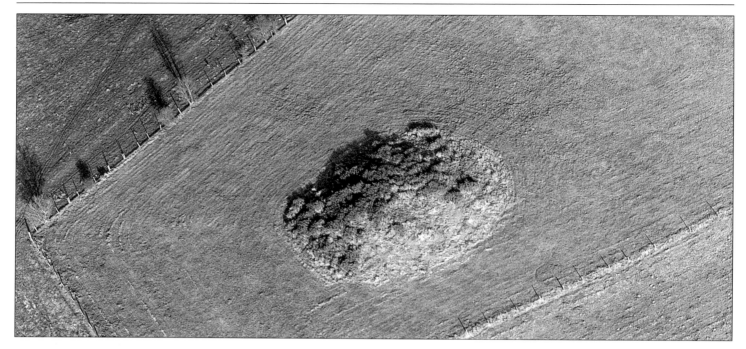

Photo 17

BRONZE AGE BARROWS AND CAIRNS

The burial mounds, or 'barrows' of the early Bronze Age (c. 2300-1400 BC) are the earliest remains of man still to be found in an upstanding form in the Shropshire landscape. Barrows are artificial mounds of earth or stone beneath which were deposited one or more human burials, either in pits, on the old ground surface or as secondary (i.e. later) interments within the body of the mound. Large numbers of barrows survive in the south-western uplands of the county - there are over twenty, for instance, on the Long Mynd. Many of them are sited on prominent ridges or hill-crests, making them visible over wide distances from the surrounding lower ground. A particularly fine example can be seen at Round Hill near Pennerley just east of Shelve (Photograph 17). Here, the well preserved mound, which has a diameter of twenty-eight metres, still stands to a height of about three metres. It probably differs little today from its appearance in the days of its first construction four thousand years ago. The apparent absence of a ditch round the base of the barrow is a feature frequently encountered in upland

stony regions, the thin soils probably inhibiting the digging of a surrounding quarry ditch to provide upcast for the mound. In fact many upland Bronze Age burial mounds were constructed wholly of stone; these are more correctly termed cairns, although they are simply a highland version of the lowland earthen barrow.

The Stiperstones ridge in south-west Shropshire (Photograph 18) has a series of cairns spread out along its summit. This prominent ridge, with its projecting tors of quartzite rock and its scree-strewn slopes covered in vast quantities of weathered stone, would have provided an ideal location for the construction of burial cairns. The largest of the cairns is visible in the foreground to the left of the path used by many thousands of walkers each year. It measures twenty one metres in diameter and stands 1.8 metres high at the centre. Beyond stands the dramatic natural outcrop known as the Devil's Chair - the highest point on the Stiperstones ridge and a target for hardy walkers at all times except the deepest days of winter.

Photo 18

Photo 19

Photo 20

CROPMARK RING-DITCHES

In the predominantly arable parts of Shropshire, such as the Upper Severn Valley, large numbers of plough-levelled round barrows can still be seen from the air as cropmarks in the form of a continuous circular ditch. These 'ring-ditches' are among the most frequently encountered of archaeological cropmarks in the county. Although some may have alternative origins and functions, the majority are probably the remains of Bronze Age round barrows (see also Photograph 17). The feature that survives as a cropmark is the surrounding quarry-ditch that would have provided soil and stone for the burial mound. Diameters can range from ten to fifty metres.

Ring-ditches occur either singly or in groups, such as those shown in Photograph 19. This group of five is situated just west of the village of Baschurch in north Shropshire, within a large arable field on the south side of the B4562 (running from left to right near the top of the picture). Within the largest ring-ditch the faint traces of a smaller and narrower inner ditch are visible, presumably a primary structural feature that would have been sealed by or encapsulated within the barrow mound. Other cropmarks in the field include a network of narrow linear features that are likely to be fossil ice-wedges, and the course of a former road crossing from right to left, joining up on the left with the modern road. This group of ring-ditches forms a small part of an early Bronze Age barrow cemetery that extended over a distance of a thousand metres or more, with outliers as far away as arable fields to the north of Baschurch. One of the latter is shown in Photograph 20, alongside the B4562 north of the village. The ring-ditch stands out prominently in relief, because of the taller growth of the cereal crop over the buried ditch of the now levelled barrow. To the right can be seen two linear features which are in fact former field boundaries, demonstrating that recent as well as ancient features can give rise to archaeological cropmarks.

Photo 21

MITCHELL'S FOLD STONE CIRCLE

Few ancient monuments have attracted such an air of mystery and fascination as the stone circles of the second and third millenium BC. These ceremonial and religious monuments of the later Neolithic and early Bronze Age are essentially features of highland Britain and hence it is in the south-west uplands of the county that the two surviving Shropshire examples are to be found. The best known is that of Mitchell's Fold, near Chirbury (centre foreground). It is located in a bleak and exposed position on the long ridge-top of Stapeley Hill and from it there are wide and spectacular views westwards over the Welsh hills. Some time around 2000-1400 BC the local Bronze Age communities erected here a circle of stones, about twenty-seven metres in diameter, consisting of thirty or so stones, although only fourteen now survive. Most of the stones stand less than a metre high, while some are mere stumps at turf level, although the tallest is almost two metres high. None seem to have been dressed. Running through the circle and to either side of it are narrow cultivation ridges whose date and relationship to the circle remain uncertain (see also Photograph 24).

Like most stone circles Mitchell's Fold probably served a ritual or ceremonial purpose. Standing today on the commanding summit of Stapeley Hill it is easy to understand why the early Bronze Age peoples of the area chose this impressive spot for the location of one of their ritual monuments.

HOARSTONE STONE CIRCLE

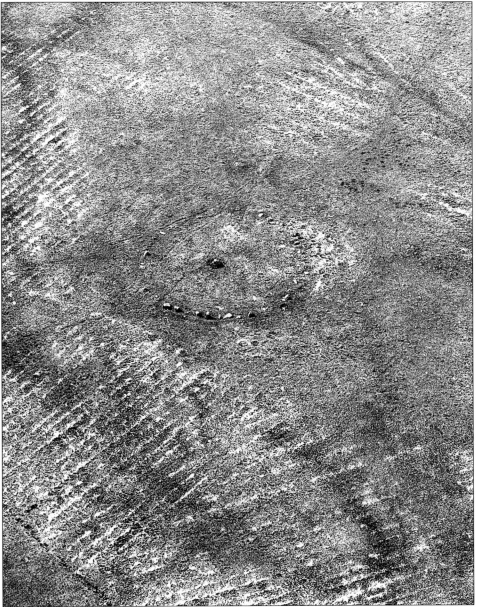

Photo 22

The Hoarstone Circle, also known as the Marsh Pool or Blackmarsh Circle, is situated on low marshy ground at the northern end of Stapeley Hill, two and a half kilometres north-east of Mitchell's Fold. The circle stands about two hundred and fifty metres from the junction of three parish boundaries; hence its name Hoarstone, which means boundary stone. Like many stone circles, this one is more properly described as oval or egg-shaped, with diameters of twenty three metres and twenty metres; it is made up of thirty-seven small stones, mostly less than knee-high, with a single stone at the centre. All the stones are of the local dolerite and none shows any signs of dressing. Detailed surveys of the site have demonstrated three significant gaps in the circle, which from the central stone align on Bromlow Callow, Stiperstones and Corndon Hill, three prominent features on the surrounding skyline. Such apparently deliberate alignments on distant landmarks, or on the rising or setting of the sun or moon, have led some to argue for an astronomical function for certain circles. The theory has not, however, met with universal acceptance. Immediately north of the circle are the low round mounds of two probable Bronze Age barrows; neither circle nor barrows have been excavated.

Two of the stones of the Hoarstone circle have had holes drilled in them on their inner faces. These have been interpreted as being significant due to their position in relation to the major axes of the circle, but a nineteenth century account describes the holes being used as "stone guns" which were fired to celebrate local weddings.

Photo 23

Photo 24

ANCIENT FIELD SYSTEMS IN SOUTH SHROPSHIRE

Through the hazy sunshine of a winter morning the outlines of a prehistoric field system come into view along the southern slopes of the Long Mynd. This remarkable series of earthworks, overlooking the Onny Valley above Plowden (Photograph 23), provides dramatic evidence for the arable exploitation of the Shropshire uplands by prehistoric farming communities. A series of interconnecting banks define an ancient field system of a type traditionally described as 'Celtic Fields'. Although these 'lynchets' have been much spread by recent ploughing they still stand up to 1.8 metres high in places, particularly on the lower slopes where the soil-depth is greater. The lynchets form a chequer pattern of square fields measuring from sixty to ninety metres across, to which access was gained by way of a double lynchet trackway. Although not yet firmly dated, the field system may well have originated during the Bronze Age, when a warmer and drier climate permitted the raising of crops on what is today a pastoral plateau. In the foreground can be seen a circular earthwork enclosure, its date and function is unknown, though it may partially overlie the lynchet banks. The utilisation of this area of the Long Mynd did not cease at the end of the prehistoric period. During the Middle Ages and Post-Medieval period it appears to have been used as a rabbit warren. The small linear 'pillow mound' visible in the centre of the photograph belongs to this phase of use, and the hedged enclosure in the distance is to this day known as 'Warren House'. Early nineteenth century

ploughing is attested by swathes of narrow ridge-and-furrow cultivation which partially overlie the circular enclosure and adjacent lynchets.

Elsewhere in the south-west uplands of Shropshire other areas of relict field systems have been discovered through aerial photography. One notable area is on Stapeley Hill, where virtually the whole of the open ridge-top is covered with the cultivation ridges of a former arable field system (Photograph 24). Along with the cultivation ridges are a number of substantial linear earth banks that run for considerable distances across the hill top. These banks frequently divide up large tracts of cultivation ridges such as those in the photograph. The actual ridges are very narrow and show none of the characteristics usually associated with medieval ridge-and-furrow, nor do they display the regularity of nineteenth century cultivation ridges. They certainly appear earlier than the trial shafts and trenches associated with the eighteenth and nineteenth century local mineral extraction industry, that are dotted across the hillside. The precise date of the ridges remains unknown but there is a possibility that they are prehistoric in origin. If this were to be the case then it would mean that large areas of the Shropshire uplands were given over to cultivation during the prehistoric period and consequently that arable farming must have formed a major part of the overall economy of the region.

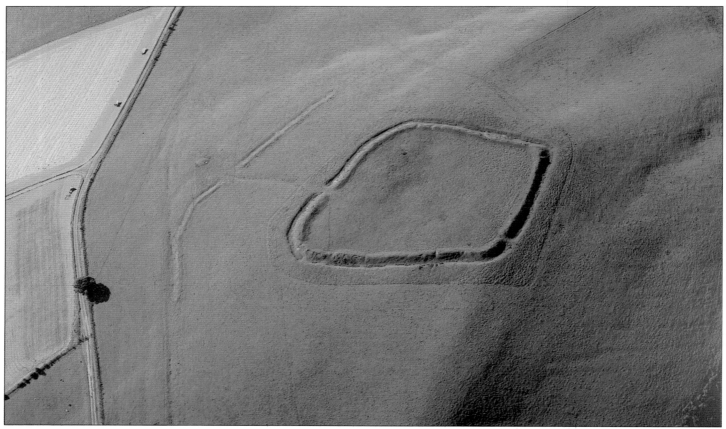

Photo 25

CAER DIN RING

Caer Din Ring is a small earthwork enclosure situated on the upland plateau of the Clun Forest. A single bank with external ditch defines a trapezoid area of just under a hectare, with an entrance on the east side. However, the defences are nowhere substantial enough to have provided an effective barrier in their present form. The evidence for the enclosure's original purpose may lie in a series of outer earthworks extending from its east side. Leading outwards from the simple entrance gap is a broad shallow holloway, or track hollowed out by traffic, leading to a ten metre break in an outward-curving earthwork some sixty metres downslope from the enclosure. This outer earthwork comprises a single bank and outer ditch and survives nowhere more than twenty centimetres in height; even allowing for plough-erosion in modern times this bank seems unlikely to have been defensive in nature. More likely these outworks were for the controlling and directing of herds of livestock into the enclosure by funnelling them along the hollow approachway and through the narrow entrance gap into the enclosure. The whole complex is perhaps best regarded as an upland prehistoric stock-corral or compound, probably constructed some time during the second or first millenium BC. As such it is an important pointer to the prehistoric pastoral economy of the region during this early period.

Photo 26

STITT HILL ENCLOSURE AND DYKES

High up on the summit of Stitt Hill, an outlying plateau of the Long Mynd, lies the prehistoric earthwork enclosure called Castle Ring. This photograph has a particular value, since it was taken before unauthorised ploughing severely damaged the earthworks. The enclosure sits at the head of a narrow ridge that projects from the plateau above steep natural slopes. The earthworks comprise a roughly triangular area, partially enclosed by a single bank and ditch and with three small linear banks across a narrow neck of land cutting off the southern approach up the ridge from the valley below. Narrow ridge-and-furrow cultivation within the enclosure probably dates to a brief episode of upland ploughing during the early nineteenth century, when many upland areas were pressed into service, and also to arable cultivation during the Napoleonic Wars.

The hilltop siting of Castle Ring has invited its classification as a hillfort, but a recent re-assessment has suggested its use as a pastoral enclosure, like Caer Din Ring in Photograph 25 associated with the control and impounding of livestock. Beyond the enclosure and extending across the ridges that slope away to left and right are two linear bank-and-ditch earthworks. These 'cross-ridge dykes' probably served as land-use divisions, defining areas of permanent pasture within which the Castle Ring stock-compound was located. A further enclosure some five hundred metres to the south (not visible in this photograph) may also have had a pastoral rather than a defensive function. The likelihood is that all these earthworks represent the remains of a landscape created by an essentially pastoral community some time in the first or second millennium BC.

IRON AGE HILLFORTS

The most spectacular of all prehistoric monuments in Shropshire are the pre-Roman hillforts, of which there are over fifty within the county. These impressive monuments are most numerous in the upland areas of south and west Shropshire, where their massive ramparts and ditches often dominate the surrounding landscape. The superbly situated hillfort of Caer Caradoc, near Chapel Lawn in south Shropshire (Photograph 27) is a stunning example.

Hillforts are defended settlements, usually sited on a hilltop, ridge-end or plateau edge; they can also be found on low ground, but even then deliberately sited with a view to commanding wide surrounding areas and utilising natural defensive features. They have traditionally been dated to the first millennium BC and in particular to the Iron Age (700 BC - AD 43), but there is increasing excavation evidence that many may have originated in the second millennium BC, during the later Bronze Age. Most of the earthworks visible today as Shropshire hillforts represent the latest phases of that particular site's development and are therefore probably Iron Age in date. Shropshire hillforts display a remarkable diversity of size, shape and complexity, ranging from relatively small forts of some one and a half hectares defended by a single bank and ditch, to massive strongholds up to twenty-eight hectares in extent, with multiple defences formed from an elaborate series of banks and ditches.

Photo 27

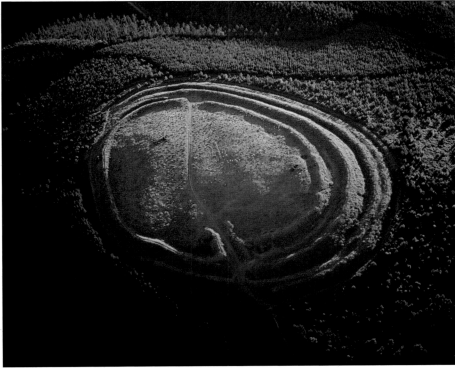

Photo 28

BURY DITCHES

The hillfort of Bury Ditches five kilometres south of Bishops Castle, is a magnificent example of a fully developed 'multivallate' hillfort, (i.e. one with more than one line of defence). On all sides its ramparts and ditches tower above steep natural slopes; from its interior extensive views are to be enjoyed in all directions. Until quite recently the whole of the hillfort was tree-covered, but severe storms in 1976 felled many of the trees and the site was then systematically cleared of timber by the Forestry Commission, revealing for the first time in decades one of the finest hillforts in Britain. It is roughly oval in shape, the defences enclosing an area of some 2.6 hectares. Around its northern side the defences comprise up to four ramparts standing as much as seven metres in height and each with an outer ditch. However, only two ramparts with an intervening ditch were provided around the southern side, where the much steeper natural slopes would have offered additional protection. Potentially the weakest parts of any hillfort's defences are its entrances. Consequently many hillforts were provided with elaborate and heavily defended entrances to deter and thwart potential attackers. One of the most common methods was the so-called 'inturned' entrance, created by extending the surrounding banks a short distance into the interior of the fort so as to create an embanked and 'inturned' passageway. The north-east (near) entrance at Bury Ditches is a fine example of this type, while the one on the far side relies on a different technique of 'overlapping' the defensive banks so as to provide flanking fire on anyone approaching the entrance. Such elaborations are an obvious demonstration that the threat of hostile attacks was real, though the frequent re-modelling of the entrances revealed by excavation at other forts may also indicate an element of display, to impress visitors at the same time as deterring attackers.

Photo 29

BURROW HILL CAMP

Hillforts were once regarded as hilltop refuges to which communities only retreated temporarily, during times of threat. However, excavations throughout England and Wales have demonstrated that many, if not most, contained permanently occupied settlements, often displaying elements of regular planning and functional zoning. Even without excavation it is sometimes possible to detect evidence of former houses or structures in hillfort interiors. Burrow Hill Camp, near Hopesay, provides such an example. Visual inspection of this impressive and well preserved multi-ramparted hillfort, either from the air or on the ground, reveals an interior pock-marked with small hollows and platforms, revealing the sites of former huts or other buildings. The hillfort itself encloses some two hectares with four lines of defence around its weaker northern circuit. The fort has clearly been enlarged and strengthened at some time, as there is a much reduced bank running across the interior and cutting off the higher parts of the hilltop. This presumably marks the limit of an earlier and smaller hillfort. Burrow Hill Camp is one of the few hillforts in the county which has a natural water supply within its ramparts - a spring in its south-west corner.

Photo 30

NORDY BANK HILLFORT

Nordy Bank is a fine example of a hillfort with a defensive circuit comprising only a single bank and ditch. It occupies a commanding spur off the lower slopes of Brown Clee Hill, eleven kilometres north-east of Ludlow. Steep slopes surround the fort on all but its eastern (right-hand) side where the ground rises to the twin summits of Abdon Burf and Clee Burf, both once crowned by hillforts which have been lost to quarrying over the past hundred years or so. Nordy Bank consists of a turf-covered rampart and rock-cut ditch enclosing an area of 2.8 hectares. The rampart is for the most part well preserved but has been breached in a number of places by small-scale quarrying which also disfigures much of the surrounding hill

slope. One original entrance survives, however, with a characteristic inturning of the rampart at either side of the entrance gap (right in photo). Internally, a square raised platform with a small square ditch on one side is visible; their date and function remains unknown. The once-thriving mining and quarrying industries of the Clee Hills have left ample evidence in the numerous spoil heaps and hollows to the right of the hillfort. The intensity of this industrial activity is further indicated by the many trackways that have etched deep holloways into the hillside as they traverse the slopes to the quarries on the summit ridge.

Photo 31

Photo 32

OLD OSWESTRY

Described by Cyril Fox as *"the outstanding work of Early Iron Age type on the Marches of Wales"*, the hillfort of Old Oswestry, on the northern outskirts of the market town from which it takes its name, is without doubt the most spectacular and impressive of Shropshire's hillforts, and one of the finest in any part of Britain. The complexity and scale of its defences more than compensate for its relatively low-lying position on the summit of a low glacial hill overlooking the Shropshire Plain to the north and west. It is roughly rectangular in plan, the defences enclosing about six hectares. A series of four banks and ditches provide the defence for most of the perimeter, but these increase to an extraordinary seven along its western side. Access to the interior was gained by two heavily defended inturned entrances, one on the west and one on the east.

On either side of the passage-like inturned western entrance (Photograph 32) are a number of deep rectangular hollows, divided by substantial banks. These are a feature, unparalleled in any other Shropshire hillfort. Many suggestions have been made about their purpose, including water-tanks, stockpens, storage pits, or simply an additional defensive feature associated with the entrance. Whatever their purpose they certainly help to make the entrance arguably the most elaborate of its kind in any hillfort in Britain. Excavations in 1939-40 showed that the hilltop was inhabited before the earthworks were built, probably during the late Bronze Age, and that the defences themselves were developed in stages of successive elaboration from about 700 BC until some time before the Roman Conquest. What is therefore seen on site today is only the latest phase in the development of a stronghold that spanned several centuries. Welsh folklore links the site with King Arthur. Indeed, one of its traditional names is Caer Ogyrfan; in Arthurian legends Ogyrfan was the father of Queen Guinevere. As yet, however, firm archaeological evidence for occupation of the hillfort in the immediate post-Roman period is lacking. During the eighth century Old Oswestry was incorporated into the line of Wat's Dyke, a Mercian frontier earthwork. The course of the Dyke stands out clearly as a straight alignment extending into the distance from the far side of the hillfort (Photograph 31).

THE BERTH

The Berth, one and a half kilometres north of Baschurch, is one of Shropshire's most unusual and intriguing ancient earthworks. It consists of two glacial mounds surrounded by an area of low-lying marshy ground. During the Iron Age each mound was enclosed by a single rampart of stone and gravel, and the two were connected by a raised causeway. A further causeway provided a link to the higher dry ground to the south. Despite its low-lying position the Berth must have been a site of considerable natural strength, for both of the fortified mounds were formerly islands within a once extensive marshland. Berth Pool, to the left of the larger mound in this photograph, is a small remnant of this former wetland area. Excavations in 1962-3 provided evidence for occupation during the middle-to-later Iron Age and again during the Roman period, but nothing that might have belonged to the site's conjectured post-Roman occupation. It has been suggested that the Berth may be the site of *Pengwern*, where the seventh-century prince of Powys, Cynddylan, had his hall. According to a series of ninth century poems known as the *Canu Llywarch Hen*, Cynddylan was defeated and killed in battle by the Saxons and his hall at Pengwern destroyed. Cynddylan is said to bave been buried at *Eglwyseu Bassa*, identified by some as the nearby Baschurch. It remains for a future generation of archaeologists to demonstrate, however, whether the Berth is truly the site of the fabled *Pengwern*.

Photo 33

Photo 34

Photo 35

CROPMARK ENCLOSURES

One of the greatest contributions of aerial survey to the archaeology of Shropshire has been its revolutionary impact on our ideas about the nature and density of prehistoric and Roman settlement in the county. The impressive prehistoric hillforts and earthwork enclosures of the region have until recently dominated the archaeological record and given rise to the concept that early settlement is largely an upland phenomenon. Over the past thirty years, however, the discovery from the air of large numbers of 'cropmark' settlements in lowland and hillslope situations has created a more balanced picture. Most of these cropmarks are probably small defended farmsteads, all above-ground traces removed by centuries of ploughing in more recent times. More than seven hundred such enclosures have been located to date, notably in the Upper Severn Valley, where their density is quite remarkable. They vary greatly in shape, though rectangular ones account for the largest single class; they usually enclose an area of about an acre. A typical example is the enclosure at Crickheath Wharf (Photograph 34), which like most of its counterparts has never been excavated but which is assumed to be of prehistoric or Romano-British date due to its similarity to dated sites elsewhere. Even where a site has not been excavated it is sometimes possible to identify internal features as cropmarks. A rare Shropshire example can be seen in an elongated quadrilateral enclosure near Culmington in south Shropshire (Photograph 35). Clearly visible within the enclosure is a smaller circle that may represent an individual house site. Beyond this enclosure and crossing the adjacent field boundary is a much larger but less distinct curvilinear enclosure, which again appears to contain internal features.

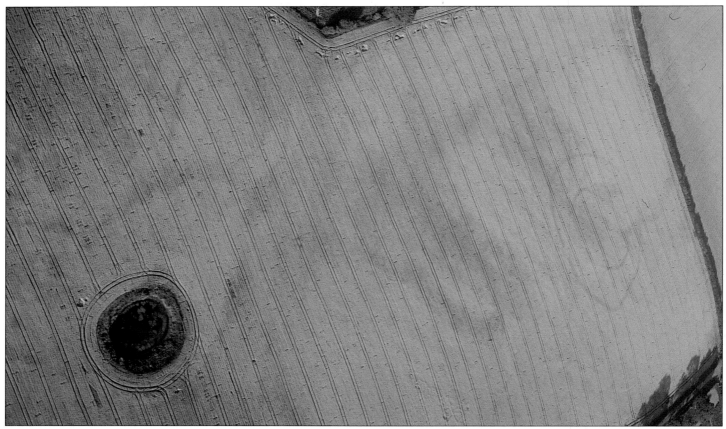

Photo 36

The clustering of enclosures such as in this example is a frequent occurrence and emphasises that these sites were once part of a complex social and geographical environment. Enclosures with more than two circuits of ditch are less frequent and often display evidence for a complicated structural history. One of the most striking of these enclosures is at Osbaston near West Felton (Photograph 37). It is sited on a low lying gravel terrace overlooking the Morda Brook. Its oval interior is defined by a triple ditch system with an inturned entrance reminiscent of those found in the major hillforts. An outer annexe partially cut through by the modern road adjoins its left side, and what may be outworks defining a funnelled approach to the entrance can also be seen. Occasionally enclosures of similar size and shape are found closely together, as at Shelvock near Ruyton XI Towns (Photograph 36), where two almost identical

enclosures lie two hundred metres apart. Both are curvilinear with widely spaced double ditches through which run simple entrance gaps. Their marked similarity may indicate a chronological, social and functional relationship between the two. Likewise at Berghill, near Whittington (Photograph 38) two similar rectangular enclosures are sited in close proximity and form elements of a cropmark complex which also includes trackways, field boundaries and other enclosures and paddocks. As with most cropmark sites only excavation would be able to elucidate the nature, development and internal relationships of a site such as this. Taken together these many hundreds of cropmark enclosures represent a richly diverse and crucially important archaeological resource for our understanding of the later prehistoric and Romano-British periods in our region.

Photo 37

Photo 38

Photo 39

ROMAN FORT AT WROXETER

The arrival of the Roman army in Shropshire during the first century AD is represented archaeologically by a series of forts and military sites, most of them visible today only as cropmarks. The earliest focal point for Roman military activity seems to have been around the present-day village of Wroxeter, eight kilometres east of Shrewsbury. From this strategic position on the banks of the River Severn there was direct access into the heart of Wales along the Upper Severn Valley. A permanent fort was established here, probably around AD 48, within five years of the first Roman landing on the south coast.

The fort is sited three hundred and fifty metres south of the village of Wroxeter, on the east bank of the Severn, overlooking and controlling an important river crossing. It is typically rectangular in shape and covers 2.2 hectares. The double-ditched defences show clearly as cropmarks, as do the central entrances in each of the fort's visible sides (the fourth - eastern - side was not under crop at the time this Cambridge University photograph was taken). To the left and right of the fort the cropmarks of other ditches may indicate annexes, or perhaps an earlier military site. The fort would have housed a five hundred strong auxiliary unit of the Roman army, perhaps a troop of Thracian cavalry to judge by a tombstone found near Wroxeter in 1725. Although pottery as late as the second century AD has been recovered from the site, the fort was probably superceded much earlier than this when a legionary fortress was established a kilometre to the north at Wroxeter about the year AD 58.

RHYN PARK

In 1976 a major Roman military base, represented by two large camps or forts, was discovered by aerial photography at Rhyn Park, near St. Martin's in north-west Shropshire. The site is one of considerable natural strength, on a plateau overlooking the steep valley of the River Ceiriog to the north and the Morlas Brook to the east. The principal camp occupies the central area of the plateau and covers a massive 19.5 hectares, sufficient to accommodate a legionary force of some six thousand men. It is rectangular in shape and its circuit is double-ditched with a third defensive ditch on the (weaker) south side. Part of the west side of the fort is visible in Photograph 40 as parallel dark-green ditches, running from top to bottom. A gap in the twin ditch system indicates the site of the original western entrance, to the left of which is a short length of ditch known as a *titulum*; with its accompanying bank. This would have served as an additional protection against attack on the gateway. The discovery of field ovens, the absence of evidence of timber building and a lack of pottery from excavations in 1977 all point to the presence of troops billeted in tented accommodation during a short campaign some time in the mid-first century AD. The fortress presumably provided a springboard for a major campaign into north Wales.

On the eastern side of the plateau are the cropmarks of a smaller, though still substantial fort of some 5.8 hectares (not visible in photograph). This partially overlies the main camp and is therefore of later date. It seems to be of a more permanent nature; its purpose was probably to control the approaches to the nearby Vale of Llangollen, for later (and ultimately successful) campaigns into the northern parts of Wales.

Photo 40

WALL TOWN FORT

Photo 41

Two miles north-east of Cleobury Mortimer, at Wall Town Farm, stands the only Roman fort in Shropshire to display still visible above-ground remains. The surviving earthworks form an almost square enclosure, with typically rounded corners, covering an area of two hectares. The earthworks are best preserved on the south (near) side where the rampart still stands two to four metres high above a wide outer ditch. The fort is bisected by the B4363 road which enters (on the right side in this photograph) through the probable site of its original east gateway. The northern half of the fort is occupied by the modern farm and its outbuildings.

A series of small-scale excavations in the 1960s showed that visible earthworks were built over an earlier phase of Roman military activity, most likely a larger fort. The surviving rampart probably dates from the early second century. Constructed of clay and originally provided with turf and timber facings, it was fronted by a ditch of V-profile that showed evidence of re-cutting on at least three occasions. At a later date a stone wall was built into the front of the rampart. To the north of the fort a now levelled annexe may have contained a civil settlement, like those which attached themselves to most Roman forts. Later Roman occupation is indicated by pottery of third and fourth century date, though the nature of this later activity is not clear. The role of the fort was probably to control the difficult upland area of the Clee Hills, and its continued occupation well into the second century indicates the importance the military authorities placed on the control of this region.

Photo 42

ROMAN MARCHING CAMP AT BROMFIELD

On campaign, the Roman army always protected itself by erecting temporary defences around its overnight camp-sites. These 'marching camps' were simple structures, consisting of an earthen bank thrown up from an external ditch and surmounted by a timber palisade. Some twenty marching camps have been recorded in Shropshire, all as aerial discoveries with no surviving traces above ground. The most intensively studied example lies at Bromfield, three kilometres north-west of Ludlow, on a gravel terrace overlooking the junction of the Rivers Teme and Onny. The ditch of the eight hectare camp is seen in this stunning Cambridge University photograph as a narrow linear cropmark defining a large rectangle, with the top left corner destroyed by recent quarrying. Also visible are the cropmark ring-ditches of prehistoric round barrows, and a small prehistoric farmstead at far right.

Excavations in advance of sand and gravel extraction showed the camp ditch to be of typical V-shaped profile. The rampart was three to three and a half metres wide and appears to have been deliberately pushed back into the ditch soon after the abandonment of the camp. In the south-east corner of the camp a series of cooking ovens had been cut into the tail of the rampart. These had been fired on several occasions, suggesting more than a simple overnight camp. Indeed, this temporary military base possibly served for a full campaigning season of several months. Despite the excavations no dating evidence has yet been found, though the camp presumably belongs to one of the numerous campaigns which the Roman army launched into Wales between AD 48 and the final conquest of Wales in about AD 75.

WHITCHURCH

The north Shropshire town of Whitchurch owes its origin to a Roman fort established on the site some time in the mid-first century AD. The town's Roman name, *Mediolanum*, or 'the place in mid-plain', admirably describes its strategic position in the Shropshire-Cheshire plain, midway between the Roman forts of Wroxeter and Chester. The main area of Roman settlement appears to have been on the hill which also accommodates the nucleus of the medieval and modern town. Indeed the present street plan may well reflect the extent of Roman settlement, particularly during the primary military phases. High Street, the wide fairway visible in the centre of the photograph, marks the principal road through *Mediolanum* and has remained the main thoroughfare of the town to this very day. At the north end stands the parish church of St Alkmund, rebuilt in 1712-13 on the site of a medieval predecessor. This marks the approximate northern line of the Roman defences. Running parallel to either side of High Street are two roads, Newtown to the left and St Mary's Street to the right; these probably mark the west and east sides of the defensive circuit.

The military occupation of Whitchurch continued until about AD 90 when the site was handed over to the civilian authorities and thereafter developed as a small town. Excavations have shown that by the end of the second century there were substantial stone buildings, and that some time after AD 170 a defensive rampart was erected around the town. By this stage *Mediolanum* had probably developed into an important market centre for the Shropshire/Cheshire plain, as it continues to be today.

Photo 43

42

Photo 44

Photo 45

POSSIBLE ROMAN SIGNAL STATIONS

Near the summit of Linley Hill, seven kilometres north-east of Bishops Castle, is a small square earthwork that may well have served as a Roman signal station (Photograph 44). The earthwork comprises a rampart six metres wide and one metre high, with an external ditch, and an internal area about twenty-one metres across. No original entrance is visible. Although no trace of internal structures or dating evidence was found during excavations in 1954, the carefully constructed rampart and the V-shaped ditch were thought by the excavator to reflect Roman military practice. The small size, however, would preclude interpretation as a Roman fort, and use as a signal station seems more feasible. The hilltop position, commanding long-distance views in all directions except to the north-east, would certainly facilitate use as part of a signalling system. One of the sight-lines could have been southward, towards the fort at Leintwardine in north Herefordshire, and another westwards to the hills south of another fort, at Brompton, some eleven and a half kilometres distant.

In 1983 a most interesting enclosure was discovered from the air on Edenhope Hill, near Mainstone, six kilometres west of Bishops Castle (Photograph 45). It was recorded by chance, soon after the field had been ploughed for the first time, and showed as a rare Shropshire example of a soilmark site. It is square in plan and small in size, measuring only about twenty metres across internally. Indeed, it bears a remarkable resemblance in both size and shape to the postulated signal station on Linley Hill. Like the Linley Hill site it also comprises a single rampart or bank, now levelled but clearly visible as a light band, with an external ditch showing as the darker surrounding zone. It is situated in an elevated position on the east slopes of Edenhope Hill with extensive views to the east, south and west. The intriguing possibility therefore arises of a sophisticated interconnected Roman military signalling system in the south-west uplands of Shropshire, of which these two sites are the surviving remnants.

Photo 46

WATLING STREET ROMAN ROAD

The most enduring traces of the Romans surviving in the landscape today are their roads, many of whose courses have continued in use for almost two thousand years. A notable example is Watling Street West which runs south-westward from Wroxeter to the Roman fort at Leintwardine. This fine Cambridge University photograph shows the course of the road, still in use today, standing out clearly as it runs along the valley of the Cound Brook before curving to enter the Church Stretton gap beyond. To the left lie the summits of Caer Caradoc and The Lawley, while to the right is the Long Mynd plateau. Typical of Roman roads, it follows a middle course through the valley away from the steep, overlooking hills. This road is likely to have been built by the Roman army in the middle years of the first century AD, and would have played a major strategic role during their conquest of Wales and the Marches.

Photo 47

Photo 48

WROXETER ROMAN TOWN

The Roman city of *Viroconium Cornoviorum* grew out of a civil settlement associated within the legionary fortress established in about AD 58 and abandoned some thirty years later. After a hesitant start the town developed by the second century into the fourth-largest town in Roman Britain, the capital of the local tribe the *Cornovii*. Unlike many Roman towns, *Viroconium* has remained virtually unencumbered by later buildings; together with the light sandy subsoil this gives excellent conditions for recording from the air the extensive cropmarks which every few summers mark out the streets and buildings of the Roman town.

Photograph 47 was taken by Professor J.K.S. St Joseph during the long, hot summer of 1975. The former streets of the town can be clearly seen, laid out in a regular grid with the cropmarks of numerous buildings in between. Many of the buildings appear to be houses ranged around central courtyards; their size and number suggest a large and prosperous urban community.

The expansion of the town probably stemmed from the visit to Britain of the Emperor Hadrian in AD 122. In the years following this the town doubled in size to about seventy-three hectares and a grandiose new civic centre was built, including a huge forum and public baths. These baths today comprise the most outstanding visible remains of the city, as can be seen graphically in Photograph 48.

By the end of the second century the city had been provided with defences totalling 3.7 kilometres in length and comprising a wide earthen bank surmounted by a wall and fronted by at least two ditches. Excavations show that after a period of decline during the fourth century a remarkable redevelopment of the civic centre took place in the mid-fifth century. This may have been the work of a local petty king, reviving the city as a regional capital after the withdrawal of Roman administration. This last phase of occupation possibly extended into the sixth century, but is likely to have ceased by the early seventh century. Thereafter, settlement seems to have been confined to the south-west corner of the former city, close to the river crossing and Anglo-Saxon church in the present village of Wroxeter (bottom left of Photograph 47).

ANCIENT LANDSCAPE NEAR CROSS HOUSES

The farmsteads and small enclosures of the prehistoric and Roman periods that today survive only as cropmarks represent but one element of the rural landscape of two thousand years and more ago. Most of these settlements would have lain within an orderly pattern of associated fields, paddocks, land boundaries and trackways. Occasionally, we can see glimpses of these broader ancient landscapes in the form of cropmarks. The accompanying photograph shows a fine example, part of a long vanished landscape extending over a distance of one and a half kilometres to the east of Cross Houses (visible at top left).

A double-ditched trackway runs across-country for a length of at least eight hundred metres. At its southern end, in the foreground, is a large rectilinear field or enclosure, and lying to either side are the ring-ditches of two Bronze Age barrows. The enclosure ditch appears to respect the position of the ring-ditches, thus suggesting that it is of a later date and that the barrows were upstanding monuments at the time of its creation. Some three hundred metres beyond the enclosure can be seen a further ring-ditch. At this point a cropmark boundary branches to the right of the trackway beyond the modern road (A458) to form part of another ditched enclosure or paddock. This extensive cropmark system is located in the Severn Valley, just three kilometres south-west of Wroxeter; we have here a small but impressive 'peephole' onto the wide-spreading rural landscape of two millennia or more ago.

Photo 49

49

Photo 50

Photo 51

OFFA'S DYKE

Winding across the upland landscape of west Shropshire like a huge snake is Offa's Dyke. Constructed during the late eighth century AD on the orders of King Offa (757-96), the monument is a testament to the power and strength of the Mercian Kingdom and of the ruler whose name it bears. The Dyke is the longest archaeological monument in Britain; Shropshire is fortunate in having within its borders some of the finest surviving sections. On the bleak elevated plateau of Llanfair Hill (Photograph 50) the Dyke can be seen at its best, as a continuous linear earthwork still standing up to two metres high, flanked on the west by a wide ditch. Here, as throughout its entire length, the Dyke is sited wherever possible to make use of west-facing slopes and vantage points looking out towards Wales. Therein lies the origin of the Dyke, as a boundary between the Kingdom of Mercia and the Welsh kingdoms to the west; the Dyke probably served both to regulate access to and from Wales and at the same time to check cross-border raids from the west. The frontier defined by this remarkable earthwork extended from the Severn Estuary, near Chepstow in the south, to the North Wales coast at Basingwerk, a distance of some two hundred and twenty-six kilometres. The sheer scale of this huge undertaking shows that this was intended as a frontier for all time. It is fitting that even today lengths of the Dyke form the national boundary between England and Wales, as for instance running north from the hamlet of Brompton, near Churchstoke (Photograph 51).

WAT'S DYKE

Wat's Dyke extends some sixty-one kilometres from the Morda Brook in north-west Shropshire to the estuary of the Dee at Basingwerk. Like its more famous counterpart Offa's Dyke, its purpose was probably to mark a boundary, most likely the north-western frontier of Mercia during the reign of Offa's predecessor, King Aethelbald (AD 716-757).

Wat's Dyke comprises a continuous bank of earth, flanked by a western ditch and sited wherever possible on west-facing slopes, looking out towards Wales. It follows a course roughly parallel to Offa's frontier but between one to six kilometres further east. Recent research suggests that Offa's Dyke may have utilised Wat's Dyke for part of its northern alignment.

Sir Cyril Fox, pioneer of Mercian Dyke studies in the 1920s, believed that Wat's Dyke terminated in north-west Shropshire, at Maesbury, four kilometres south of Oswestry. In recent years, however, aerial photography has demonstrated its southward continuation, as a continuous linear cropmark aligned on the earthwork sections north of Maesbury. This view shows a long stretch of this cropmark west of Morton Hall, running from bottom to top across the arable fields as far as the road in the middle distance. Thereafter its course is followed by modern hedgelines all the way to Oswestry in the far distance.

Excavations have confirmed the cropmark as the filled-in ditch of Wat's Dyke, the bank here completely levelled by ploughing in recent centuries. As a result of these discoveries we can now see that Wat's Dyke originally extended perhaps three and a half kilometres south of Maesbury crossing low-lying marshy ground to join the Morda Brook, just north of the village of Maesbrook.

Photo 52

TIMBER HALLS AT FROGMORE, ATCHAM

Photo 53

Perhaps one of the most remarkable of Shropshire's cropmark sites was discovered by Cambridge University air photographers in the hot dry summer of 1975. On a gravel ridge at Frogmore, a kilometre south of Upton Magna but within the northern part of the parish of Atcham, was recorded a complex of marks comprising a series of overlapping enclosures, trackways and linear features (centre of photograph, either side of the modern road). The filled-in former course of the Shropshire Union Canal survives as a broad curving cropmark to the right of the road. But the most striking elements of the whole complex are what seem to be the foundations of two long timber buildings, left of and parallel to the road. One of the buildings has been partly destroyed by a gravel pit.

Unique within Shropshire, these remarkable buildings are strikingly similar to the Anglo-Saxon timber halls at Yeavering in Northumberland, shown by excavation to be seventh century 'royal' halls of the Northumbrian kings. Of the Frogmore examples the larger measures some twenty-four metres in length; both are about six metres wide. At each end the buildings have characteristically narrow porches. If the cropmarks do indeed represent Anglo-Saxon 'royal' halls then they are one of the most important archaeological discoveries in the whole county, and a vital clue to our understanding of the expansion of the Mercian kingdom into the Upper Severn Valley during the seventh century AD.

ST. EATA'S CHURCH, ATCHAM

Standing picturesquely on the eastern bank of the River Severn, and overlooking the bridges that cross the river just to its north, is the church of St. Eata at Atcham. A familiar landmark to motorists along the old A5, the church is also one of the most ancient and historically important in Shropshire. It was here in 1075 that Ordericus Vitalis, the monk who wrote a history of the Normans, was baptised as a child; part of the present church would have been standing at that very time. Indeed, the nave of the church is wholly of Anglo-Saxon build and may even date from as early as the seventh or eighth century AD. Its walls are built entirely of re-used building stone from the nearby Roman city at Wroxeter, and in its north wall an original pre-Conquest window still survives intact. The large and impressive tower dates to about 1200, while the chancel was erected some time in the thirteenth century.

Perhaps the most intriguing aspect of the church is its unique dedication to St. Eata, a Northumbrian monk, who was Abbot of Hexham and Bishop of Lindisfarne, and who died in 685. It is tempting to see this unusual dedication as the direct result of a personal visit to the area by Eata, perhaps even under the patronage of the occupants of the 'royal halls' at nearby Frogmore. Whatever the origin of the church, there can be little doubt of its importance as one of the earliest surviving buildings in Shropshire.

Photo 54

Photo 55

CHIRBURY: AN ANGLO-SAXON 'BURH'

In AD 915 Aethelflaed, Lady of the Mercians, constructed a 'burh' or fortified enclosure at a place called *Cyricbyrig*. This is believed by many to be the village of Chirbury, two and a half kilometres east of Offa's Dyke at the head of the Rea and Camlad valleys, both of which offer direct and easy access to the Upper Severn valley and thereby into the heart of Wales. No doubt this strategic location dictated the siting of the 'burh' here, presumably to deter Viking incursions into the Upper Severn Valley. A rectangular earthwork butting onto the road at the top right of the photograph has been suggested as the site of this 'burh'; but excavations there in 1958 proved inconclusive, showing no evidence to date or explain the defences. A closer study of the core of the village, however, shows it to be laid out on a markedly rectilinear plan, perhaps reflecting the original form and location of the 'burh'. The large and impressive church of St. Michael was an Anglo-Saxon minster church, and mother-church for a huge parish throughout the Middle Ages. Its foundation must date back at least to the beginning of the tenth century, as the existence of a church at this time is clearly indicated in the place-name *Cyricbyrig* which means 'church fort'. Around 1200 the church became a priory for Augustinian canons, being rebuilt to serve the needs of both priory and parish. Unfortunately, only a tiny fragment of the monastic range of the Priory survives to the present day.

WESTBURY

The presence of Anglo-Saxon burhs along the western margin of Shropshire may be indicated by a number of settlements with place-names containing the element 'bury'. One such example is Westbury, where the modern road system, which defines a D-shaped enclosure in the centre of the village, may reflect the course of a former fortification. The church of St. Mary stands within this enclosure; like its equivalent at Chirbury, it was the head of a large medieval parish. Its origin as an Anglo-Saxon minster is suggested by the record of two priests resident at Westbury in 1086. The settlement is sited on the line of the principal Roman road from a fort near Montgomery to the town of Wroxeter; here the road can be seen extending in a straight line far into the distance to the east. Westbury also lies at the junction of several other routes into Wales, including the ridgeway over the Long Mountain. Consequently this would have been a potentially important strategic location for a 'burh'. A further hint comes from the entry in the Anglo-Saxon Chronicle for the year 1053 which records the killing of many English frontier guards by Welshmen at a place called *Waestbyrig*, perhaps the now-peaceful Shropshire village of Westbury.

Photo 56

Photo 57

CASTLE PULVERBATCH

The arrival of the Normans in Shropshire soon after 1066 brought with it that most familiar of all monuments of the Middle Ages – the castle. From these strongholds – built first in timber but later in stone - political and military control was effectively and ruthlessly enforced. The large number of castles in Shropshire illustrates the Normans' determination to stamp their control and authority over this strategically important region. The castles of the Conquest period (before about 1100) were largely constructed of earth and timber and were mainly of the 'motte and bailey' type. One of the most impressive examples lies at Pulverbatch, twelve kilometres south-west of Shrewsbury. Castle Pulverbatch is sited in a position of considerable natural strength on a ridge overlooking a valley through which passed the main medieval road from Shrewsbury to Bishops Castle. Here, the motte, a circular conical mound of earth,

stands eight and a half metres high; its summit would originally have carried a tall timber tower at its centre, with a perimeter palisade around its edge. The base of the motte is surrounded by a defensive ditch which effectively cuts it off from two attached and conjoined rectangular baileys or defended enclosures. Access from the baileys to the motte would have been by way of a wooden drawbridge. The baileys are each defended by a substantial earth bank, which would have carried a timber palisade, and by an outer defensive ditch. Within them would have stood a series of timber buildings, including a hall, chapel, stables, stores and quarters. The castle may have been erected by Roger Venator, who held the manor in 1086, though it is not until about 1153 that it is first mentioned in surviving texts of the period.

Photo 58

CAMP RING, CULMINGTON

The magnificent motte and bailey castle known as Camp Ring, near Culmington in lower Corvedale, has no surviving contemporary medieval references to either its history or its owners, but this is more than balanced by the castle's superb state of physical preservation. It stands on a low ridge above water-meadows between the River Corve and Pye Brook. Its circular motte, just over two metres high, is surrounded by a wide ditch which may originally have been water-filled. The attached circular bailey measures fifty metres in diameter and is enclosed by a five metre wide bank and outer ditch. The original entrance can be seen as a gap through the bailey bank at bottom right. To the left of the motte are two contiguous rectangular enclosures defining an L-shape, one of which contains a rectangular depression, probably a former fishpond. These enclosures may have been additional baileys attached to the castle; at first appearance they give the impression of being later than the distinctive ridge-and-furrow field system that lies within and around them. Indeed the castle is wholly surrounded by exceptionally well-preserved cultivation ridges of presumed medieval date; together with the castle these make Camp Ring one of the most impressive earthwork complexes in the county of Shropshire.

A 'LOST' CASTLE AT ACTON BANK

A rare example of a motte and bailey castle, visible only as a cropmark, lies at Acton Bank, near Bishops Castle. On a ridge above the hamlet of Acton stands an almost levelled mound, once two metres high and until recently interpreted as a Bronze Age barrow. However, in 1981 the surrounding field was ploughed and put down to barley. As the crop ripened later that summer the true nature of the site became apparent through air photography. The cropmark of a wide ditch surrounding the mound is strikingly obvious in this 1986 photograph of the site. Furthermore, joining onto this is a D-shaped enclosure defining what appears to be a small bailey attached to the mound. The original entrance to the bailey can be seen as a centrally placed gap in its flanking ditches. A second but smaller enclosure on the left of the picture may be an associated outer bailey. Few sites better illustrate the contribution of aerial archaeology to the understanding and interpretation of known archaeological monuments.

Photo 59

Photo 60

CLUN CASTLE

Probably founded some time in the late eleventh century, Clun Castle is today one of the finest and most impressive castles of the Welsh Marches. A huge oval motte, with two baileys, overlooks the tree-lined meanders of the River Clun. The smaller bailey, to the left of the motte, is today used as a bowling green. The most striking feature of the castle, however, is its huge - though ruinous - late thirteenth century Great Tower, its four storeys still standing some twenty-five metres high. The sheer scale and size of the tower demanded its construction into the side of the motte, rather than on the summit. Extensive remains of the castle's perimeter wall, and two circular towers, also survive on the motte. First mentioned in about 1140, the castle was attacked and burned by the Welsh in 1195-6 and later besieged by King John in 1216. From about 1155 until 1549 it was held as the principal castle of

the Barony of Clun by the FitzAlans, the greatest landowners and most important family in Shropshire throughout the Middle Ages.

To the right of the river on low lying ground below the castle, is an unusual complex of earthworks, probably the remains of a medieval 'pleasance' or pleasure garden and an attached complex of fishponds. The 'pleasance' itself would have stood within the square moated enclosure and would have consisted of one or more pavilions ranged around a central formal garden. The adjacent banks and depressions represent the former fishponds, like the 'pleasance' providing for the needs of the nearby castle. This unusual survival emphasises the role of the medieval castle as a private residence as well as a military stronghold, in this case belonging to one of the great baronial families of medieval England.

HEATH FARM, AMASTON

Not all earth-and-timber castles of the early Norman period were of the motte and bailey type. Another variant is known as the 'ringwork'. Ringworks are enclosures defended by a substantial bank and outer ditch, and are usually, but not always, circular in shape. They often have a tower or gatehouse defending the entrance but have no mound or artificial motte. A fine ringwork can be seen at Heath Farm, Amaston, eleven kilometres west of Shrewsbury. The ringwork itself consists of a circular earthwork thirty-one metres in diameter, with a bold perimeter bank. It overlooks an attached bailey (above and to the right) that is simply a low rectangular platform with no surviving trace of enclosing bank or outer ditch. The junction between ringwork and bailey has been obliterated by the approach road to the adjacent Heath Farm. The farmhouse dates to about 1800 and is the sole surviving remnant of the former medieval hamlet of Amaston. Extending over a wide area to the south and east of the ringwork are the well-preserved ridge-and-furrow earthworks of an open-field system that belonged to the medieval settlement. In 1086 seven tenants were recorded at Amaston, but only four remained by 1379; despite this, Amaston may have survived as a recognisable hamlet until the 1690s. The manor was part of the barony of Montgomery, and in the thirteenth century was said to be held in return for providing two footmen for forty days in times of war.

Photo 61

Photo 62

MOTTE AND BAILEY CASTLE AT MORE

These impressive remains of a seemingly typical motte and bailey castle are situated at More, three kilometres north-east of Bishops Castle. In fact excavation has shown the motte to have developed from an earlier ringwork, through the infilling and raising of the interior to form a mound. Extending from the base of the mound is a sub-rectangular inner bailey containing well-preserved building-platforms. A broad holloway cuts through a second but larger outer bailey which is defined by scarp slopes and a bank at its right-hand corners. The holloway runs for a further two hundred metres until it joins the modern road through the village of More, just visible at the right. A curving length of bank against the modern road may be the last surviving trace of a third and even larger outer bailey.

The present village is centred on the small Norman church of St. Bartholomew; both castle and village were probably laid out as a single unit some time in the late eleventh or early twelfth century, when it was carved out of the large Anglo-Saxon estate of Lydbury North. The distinct curving field boundary beyond the castle earthworks may define the boundary of this early 'plantation'.

Although little is known of the castle's history it is recorded that in the time of Henry I (1100-1135) the Lord of More was required to command two hundred foot soldiers whenever the King of England crossed into Wales in time of war. He was to march in the vanguard of the army and personally carry the King's standard. The castle earthworks at More provide a fitting reminder of the status and prestige of one of Shropshire's noble lords during the Middle Ages.

Photo 63

WHITTINGTON CASTLE

A castle at Whittington is first mentioned in 1138, when it was fortified by William Peverel against King Stephen. The castle originated as an earth-and-timber castle of motte and bailey type, but was later extensively altered and adapted during the thirteenth century, when it was rebuilt in stone. In 1204 the manor and castle of Whittington passed into the hands of Fulk Fitz Warin III, whose family continued to hold it until 1420. In 1221 Fulk was given licence to fortify the castle, 'as much as was essential to protect it from the Welsh.'

The main feature of the new castle was a rectangular inner bailey encapsulating an earlier twelfth century motte. This inner bailey was encircled by a stone curtain wall, with projecting semi-circular towers at its four corners; the north-west angle tower, still largely intact, also served as a gatehouse into the inner bailey. Entry into the outer bailey of the castle was gained through a tall twin-towered gatehouse, which now faces onto the road through the village, giving thousands of travellers each year a vivid impression of the castle's original grandeur.

The castle's outer defence, on its south and west sides (background in the photograph) comprises three concentrically arranged banks, each fronted by a once water-filled ditch. In fact the most striking feature of the thirteenth century castle would undoubtedly have been the wide-scale use of water in its defences. Both the inner and outer baileys were completely surrounded by water, creating self-contained defensive units. The water-filled moat that survives today alongside the old A5 road is only a small remnant of the once extensive sheets of water that protected the castle against attackers seven hundred years ago.

CAUS CASTLE & MEDIEVAL BOROUGH

At the east end of the Long Mountain, on a prominent hill overlooking the valley route from Shrewsbury to Montgomery, stands the deserted castle-cum-borough of Caus. It was founded some time early in the twelfth century by Roger Fitz Corbet, who named his new foundation after the Pays de Caux in Normandy, the Corbet place of origin. The castle was superbly sited on the highest point of the ridge, wooded in this 1990 aerial view. It comprises a huge motte, surrounded by a deep rock-cut ditch, and with traces of a stone shell-keep on its summit. An attached inner bailey contains a well and the substantial remains of two towers and a gateway. By 1200 a town or 'borough' had been established within the large outer bailey of the castle. In this year Caus was granted a market charter followed in 1248 by the right to hold an annual fair. The borough had its own chapel of St. Margaret, founded in 1272, and by 1349 there were fifty-eight burgesses living there. By the end of the fourteenth century, however, the town was beginning to show signs of decay, and this was further aggravated in 1444 when many of its buildings were burnt down during the rebellion of Sir Griffith Vaughan. A survey of 1521 paints a sad picture of decay in both castle and town, and the site was finally abandoned in the early seventeenth century. Little now survives of the medieval borough, other than the huge ramparts that served as the town's defences. As late as the nineteenth century the street pattern was said to be still discernible, but the only semblance of this today is the solitary holloway leading up the hill and through the now crumbling gateway into the town.

Photo 64

Photo 65

GADLAS MOAT

One of the most frequently encountered of all medieval monuments in the Shropshire landscape is the so-called 'moated site'. Over one hundred and seventy are known in Shropshire, with a particularly dense concentration in the north of the county. Essentially these were domestic sites, for the most part manor houses and farmsteads wholly or partially enclosed by a water-filled ditch. They are usually found on low-lying land like that of the North Shropshire plain. The finely preserved moat at Gadlas, on Dudleston Heath near Ellesmere, is in many ways a typical example. A ten metre wide ditch, still partially water-filled, defines a rectangular area of approximately

half a hectare. Access to the interior was gained along a causeway, centrally placed across the eastern (near) arm of the moat. The curving ditch in front of the moat is a former stream course, which may have provided a readily available water supply for the moat. Within the interior, or 'island' as it is known, there would have stood a range of buildings. Gadlas, like most moated sites, was probably constructed during the thirteenth or early fourteenth century, a time of economic expansion when freehold farmers were colonising the ill-drained marginal lands of north Shropshire and bringing them into cultivation for the first time (a process known as 'assarting').

BLAKEMERE CASTLE

The moated site known as Blakemere Castle stands one and a half kilometres north-east of Whitchurch. It accommodated the manor house of the Le Strange family, who first acquired the manor in the early twelfth century. It passed into the hands of the Talbots during the fourteenth century, and in 1383 became the birthplace of John Talbot, the first Earl of Shrewsbury and hero of the Hundred Years War with France (1361-1453). The Talbot family sold the manor in 1590 and by 1695 the manor house was said to be *'quite ruined'*. The earthwork remains of the manor house are sited in a prominent position overlooking Blakemere Pool, from which it takes its name. The surrounding moat, partially filled and now dry, encloses a rectangular 'island' that is raised above the level of the surrounding fields. A number of narrow trenches visible on the island are the remnants of small-scale archaeological excavations in 1963, while the irregular form of the left side has been created by soil quarrying in modern times.

Although the construction of a moat around a homestead would have provided a measure of security and protection it seems increasingly likely that the principal motivation may have been the moat as a status symbol. Perhaps constructed as a conscious imitation of the defended castle, the moat would have been seen as a desirable feature by the newly emerging middle classes of medieval England.

Photo 66

Photo 67

MOATED SITE AT COURT HOUSE, GRETTON

As elsewhere in Britain, most Shropshire moats are simple rectangular 'islands' surrounded by a single wide ditch. However, a notable exception can be seen at Court House, Gretton, near Cardington, one of only two examples in the county of a 'concentric' or multi-ditched moat. A small square moat, seen in the centre of the picture, is surrounded by a much larger and irregular outer moat which opens out on its south (left) side into what was originally an artificial lake. Other features of note include a small rectangular fishpond within the bottom right corner of the inner moat, and another just outside it but connected to it by a shallow ditch.

Extensive remains of ridge-and-furrow ploughing surround the site. The extent and complexity of the earthwork suggest a site of some importance, yet remarkably there are no references to a manor house or other significant residence here during the Middle Ages. More recently it has been suggested that the earthworks may be those of a post-medieval formal garden. However there is equally no mention of a major house in the area with which the earthworks could have been associated. Thus the real dating and function of this remarkable complex remains unresolved.

Photo 68

STOKESAY CASTLE

Stokesay Castle is one of the finest thirteenth century manor houses in England and arguably the most picturesque of Shropshire's ancient monuments. Despite its name Stokesay is in fact a fortified manor house rather than a true castle. It is largely the work of Lawrence of Ludlow, who owned it between 1281 and 1296. Lawrence was the greatest wool merchant of his day and in 1291 was granted a licence from Edward I to fortify his house at Stokesay. The result was a residence of considerable size and elegance, surrounded by a water-filled moat, now dry, but originally fed from a nearby pool. Within the courtyard, and along its west (far) side, was the main residential block, which still survives complete. It consists of a magnificent hall and 'solar' (living room) between two defensive towers. The north (right-hand) tower is

the earlier of the two, probably built in about 1240. Entry into the courtyard is through an elaborately timber-framed gatehouse opposite the residential block, built in the seventeenth century on the site of a medieval predecessor.

During the Civil War Stokesay Castle was garrisoned by the Royalists but surrendered to Parliament in 1645. Although the castle escaped almost unscathed from this encounter the adjacent church of St. John the Baptist suffered extensive damage during a battle in the following year. Consequently the church was virtually rebuilt in 1654, giving it a particular interest and importance as one of the few churches built in England during the Commonwealth period.

Photo 69

KNOCKIN: A 'PLANTED' VILLAGE

Many Shropshire villages of medieval origin were deliberately laid out as 'plantations' and the evidence for this still survives in the plans of such villages, with their regular road patterns and property boundaries. Frequently these planned settlements are closely associated with castles; in these instances they were probably developed and regulated by the lord of the manor as settlements integral with the castle.

The village of Knockin provides an excellent example, especially when seen from the air. With its distinct linear form strung out along either side of the road, and with parallel tenement plots extending at right angles to it, there can be little doubt that this is a medieval plantation. A castle was established here between 1154 and 1160 by Guy Le Strange and Knockin was to remain the principal holding or 'caput' of the Le Strange barony for most of the Middle Ages. The castle mound still survives in the rectangular wood at the far (east) end of the village. Immediately in front of the tree-covered mound is the small parish church of St. Mary, founded between 1182 and 1195; its present structure largely dates to this period. The church may originally have stood within an outer bailey of the castle. The village itself was then laid out along what was the main road from Shrewsbury to Oswestry during the Middle Ages. There is no mention of a settlement at Knockin in the Domesday Survey of 1086, and it seems therefore that the castle, church and village are all a creation of the second half of the twelfth century, carved out of the earlier Anglo-Saxon manor of Osbaston.

Photo 70

HODNET

Hodnet, eight kilometres south-west of Market Drayton, is another village with a layout that displays evidence of regulated medieval planning. In Anglo-Saxon times Hodnet was already an important settlement, the administrative centre for much of north-east Shropshire, an area known as the 'Hundred' of Hodnet. The nucleus of this early settlement probably centred on the church and adjacent road junction (centre right of the photograph). The church of St. Luke contains no fabric earlier than the fourteenth century, though the foundation is certainly of greater antiquity, a church at Hodnet being recorded as early as 1086.

Some time during the late eleventh or early twelfth century a motte and bailey castle was erected at Hodnet. Extensive earthwork remains of this castle survive within the tree covered area lower-left

of the church. This same wooded area is bounded to its right by a road along which the older parts of the village extend in a linear form from an original nucleus near the church. This linear extension bears all the hallmarks of a deliberately laid out part of the village. In 1264 Odo de Hodnet, the manorial lord, was granted the right to hold a weekly market and annual fair at Hodnet; it may be this that provided the stimulus for the distinctively planned extension to the settlement. Hodnet Hall (top centre of the photograph) is a fine country house, built in 1870 to replace an earlier seat of the Vernon family. The Hall and its beautiful gardens and grounds lie within a former park of the medieval lords of Hodnet. Indeed, the present Hall is the eventual successor to the castle whose foundation began the Norman and Medieval expansion of the village.

Photo 71

COLD WESTON DESERTED MEDIEVAL VILLAGE

Situated at a height of two hundred and sixty metres on the lower slopes of the Clee Hills is the deserted medieval village of Cold Weston. Today all that survives - in terms of buildings - is a solitary cottage and a church, surrounded by extensive earthworks representing the road, houses and fields of the now vanished medieval village. The tiny two-cell church of St. Mary, within the circular copse at the centre of this photograph, is largely twelfth century in date. Leading from the church to the road on the right is the holloway of a former road, flanked by platforms representing the sites of former houses. Elsewhere scarps and terraces define paddocks and small enclosures, while surrounding the whole complex are the remains of an extensive ridge-and-furrow field system.

Cold Weston is first recorded in 1090, but the village declined rapidly during the fourteenth century. In 1341 the parish was valued at only 4s 3d, compared to £5.3s.0d in 1291. It was then said to be a *'waste place'* where there had once been an abundance of cattle, but which had long been decreasing due to the *'murrain'* (pestilence) which prevailed in the area. There were only two tenants, both in great want, and others had absconded. In the same year the Chapel was presented in turn to four parsons, but each refused it.

This stark picture of dereliction and poverty is found repeatedly among the agricultural communities of the region during the fourteenth century. Climatic deterioration, failed harvests, pestilence, high taxation and plagues precipitated an agricultural decline. In the face of such factors it is easy to understand the decline and desertion of a hamlet like Cold Weston, its very name reflecting the harsh and bleak location on an exposed north-facing hillside.

Photo 72

MEDIEVAL SHRUNKEN SETTLEMENTS

The decline and contraction of medieval settlements did not always lead to their total desertion. Equally often the nucleated village or hamlet merely shrunk in size, sometimes to no more than a single farm. Where this happened earthworks often betray the original form and extent of the settlement, for example at Aston Botterell in south-east Shropshire (Photograph 72). Among the extensive earthworks that survive in and around the present settlement is an ovoid ringwork with attached annexes, in the field to the top left of the medieval parish church. This is almost certainly the site of the medieval manor house - its antiquity shown by the way the road bends to respect its position. In the field to the top right of the ringwork further earthworks probably represent crofts and paddocks, showing that the settlement was formerly larger and more nucleated than it is today. The name Aston means 'east settlement' and probably refers to its situation east of Brown Clee Hill. The suffix 'Botterell' derives from the Boterel family who were lords of the manor from the thirteenth century onwards. In 1263 Thomas Boterel received a charter for a weekly market and an annual three day fair in his manor of Aston. But by 1341 there were no sheep in the parish, the land lay untilled, and certain poor tenants had withdrawn through poverty. This decline in the fortunes of the manor undoubtedly led to the shrinkage of the village, so vividly represented in this aerial view of its remaining earthworks. About three kilometres south of Aston Botterell lies another shrunken settlement, at Norton (Photograph 73). Today only a single farm marks what in 1086 was a village of eleven tenants, in the possession of Rainald, the Sheriff of Shropshire. As at nearby Aston Botterell the remnant earthworks of platforms, holloways, paddocks and ridge-and-furrow cultivation surround the modern farm and provide clear evidence for the former extent of the settlement. In the Domesday Survey Norton was accounted as a manor in its own right, but by 1255 it had been annexed to the manor of Aston Botterell, within which parish it still lies to this day.

Photo 73

Photo 74

Photo 75

Photo 76

MEDIEVAL FIELD SYSTEMS

During the Middle Ages the 'open-field' system of arable farming was widely practised throughout Shropshire. Essentially this was a communal arrangement in which farmers held individual strips of land scattered throughout large open fields surrounding the settlement. The most distinctive surviving evidence of these medieval fields is the so-called 'ridge-and-furrow', creating a corrugated surface which is a familiar sight wherever medieval arable has since remained in pasture. Photograph 74 shows an expanse of splendid ridge-and-furrow round the medieval hamlet of Burley, in Corvedale, now shrunk to the size of a single farm. The deliberate ploughing of strips within the open fields into one or more narrow raised 'ridges', separated by linear depressions or 'furrows', is believed to have aided surface drainage and hence increased crop yields. A distinguishing feature of medieval ridge-and-furrow is a tendency to curve in the form of a reversed 'S', so clearly evident in the fields at Burley. This is likely to have been in order to permit a large plough team of oxen to turn before the end of the ridge was reached without damaging the adjacent land. At Burley this characteristic curvature became fossilised in the present-day hedgelines which follow the course of their medieval predecessors.

The extent of arable cultivation in north-west Shropshire during the medieval and post-medieval periods is dramatically illustrated in Photograph 75, which shows vast areas of ridge-and-furrow cultivation covering hundreds of hectares along the low-lying flanks of the River Vyrnwy between Llanymynech and Melverley. A light covering of snow has here thrown the ridges into relief with stunning effect.

'Strip-lynchets' are another feature of the medieval landscape. These are artifical cultivation terraces consisting of a long flat strip above a steeply-scarped edge or 'lynchet', often standing to a considerable height. They occur most typically on steep hillsides where the lynchets either run parallel to the contours or diagonally across them. Photograph 76, shows a fine series of cross-contour lynchets on a hillside overlooking the River Redlake near Bucknell. The broad curving banks represent the lynchet scarps while on the terraces themselves can be seen the traces of typical ridge-and-furrow cultivation. These strip-lynchets are simply an adaptation of the normal medieval open fields onto steep ground. Their survival over large areas of the south Shropshire uplands bears witness to the ability of the medieval farmers to push the limits of arable production far beyond the lowland open-field systems, into areas rarely cultivated in the succeeding centuries.

MIDDLETON HILL PILLOW MOUNDS

This strange cross-shaped mound on the bracken covered slopes of Middleton Hill, near Chirbury, is one of Shropshire's more unusual historic earthworks. It is an artificial rabbit warren of a type known as a pillow mound. These regular-shaped mounds of earth were raised for rabbits in areas where the ground was too rocky for the animals to burrow. This cruciform example stands half a metre in height, has a gently rounded top, and arms twenty metres in length surrounded by a shallow ditch. Typically, it is sited on sloping ground to assist with the drainage. A number of other mounds can be seen at top right; it is quite usual for mounds to be grouped together in this way. Among this group there are two long rectangular examples, the most common shape, one being partially cut by a trackway; the group also contains a circular mound.

Artificial rabbit warrens were constructed from the Middle Ages until the eighteenth century. In addition to providing a welcome supplement to the table, rabbits also brought a measure of profitability to otherwise unproductive land. Whether the warrens on Middleton Hill are medieval in origin is not known, though the large cruciform mound was evidently recut in 1887 and turves from the surrounding ditch banked up on the mound.

Photo 77

79

MONTFORD FISH WEIR

The island in the bend of the River Severn at Montford, six kilometres west of Shrewsbury, is the site of a fish weir that was in existence by the late eleventh century. The original course of the Severn follows the right-hand river channel in this view and across this was constructed the now-vanished weir. These weirs usually extended across the river from bank to bank and consisted of a stout fence of stakes from which were suspended fish traps in the form of long wicker baskets. Although not solid barriers they would nevertheless have provided a serious obstacle to river navigation. To overcome this problem an artificial bypass, known as a 'bylet', was frequently created (the left-hand channel in this photograph). This produced an artificial island alongside the weir, as is so clearly the case at Montford. The Montford fishery is first mentioned in 1086, when it was split between the two manors of Montford and Ford. In 1575 a special commission recorded the Montford weir as one of forty on the Shropshire Severn. Although most had been abandoned by the end of the seventeenth century the Montford fish weir remained in use until late in the nineteenth century, one of the last to survive in active use in the county of Shropshire.

Photo 78

ALBERBURY CASTLE AND CHURCH

Photo 79

The village of Alberbury, thirteen kilometres west of Shrewsbury, is mostly a creation of the late eighteenth century, bearing little resemblance to its appearance during the Middle Ages. Despite this there are two important medieval survivals - the church and the castle.

The church of St. Michael (centre) is a large and imposing structure containing much medieval fabric. First mentioned in the mid-twelfth century, the church is likely to have its origin in an Anglo-Saxon minster church and was still being served by four priests as late as the thirteenth century. The earliest surviving part of the church is the imposing tower of about 1300. Its most distinctive feature is a steep saddle-back roof, unique in Shropshire, as is the tower's unusual position to the north-east of the nave. Also of note is the Loton Chapel, on the south (near) side of the nave; this dates from about 1320-30 and is one of the finest fourteenth century structures in the county.

Immediately adjacent to the church on its south (near) side are the remains of Alberbury Castle, probably built by Fulk Fitz Warin III in the early thirteenth century. Its remains comprise a rectangular keep which originally contained a first-floor hall. The keep occupies the south-west angle of a polygonal enclosure, defined and enclosed by a 'curtain wall' still standing in parts almost three metres in height. In 1223 the castle was attacked and taken by Llywelyn the Great, Prince of Wales, and was not regained by Fitz Warin until 1226. By the sixteenth century the castle was ruinous, the antiquary John Leland writing of *"the ruins of Fulk Guarine, the noble warrior's castle"*.

MELVERLEY CHURCH

Few Shropshire churches have a siting so dramatic as that of St. Peter's church at Melverley. Perched on the right bank of the River Vyrnwy near its confluence with the Severn, its setting is at once both picturesque and precarious. Moreover, the church itself has a special importance as a rare example of a timber-framed church of medieval date – one of only two in Shropshire. It consists of a simple rectangle accommodating both nave and chancel and probably dating to the late fifteenth century; on the south side is a slightly later sixteenth century porch. The bellcote dates to 1718. The whole structure is built of close-set vertical timbers with rendered lath-and-plaster infill. Internally, the church is divided into three parts by stout wooden frames, one of which supports a west gallery erected in 1718. Although the church was heavily restored in 1878 and again in 1924-5, it still survives almost unchanged from its appearance when first built in the late Middle Ages.

During 1991 a major programme of stabilisation was carried out to consolidate and protect the church from collapse into the River Vyrnwy. The erosion of the river bank had advanced to such an extent that the foundations of the church were in danger of being undermined. The remedial work was successfully completed, ensuring the survival of this fascinating and beautiful building, an architectural gem of truly national importance.

Photo 80

Photo 81

BATTLEFIELD CHURCH

The church of St. Mary Magdalene, Battlefield, was founded in 1406 as a collegiate church and chantry chapel for the souls of those slain in the Battle of Shrewsbury, fought three years earlier between the royal army of Henry IV and the rebel forces of Sir Henry Percy. In the ensuing royal victory up to nine thousand men are reputed to have lost their lives; the church itself is said to stand over a mass grave on the very field of battle. The foundation charter granted by Henry IV made the rector of nearby Albright Hussey warden of the chapel, with the right to nominate five chaplains. The chapel was completed within three years, although the tower was added later and was not completed until the early sixteenth century. No traces now survive of the college buildings that once stood adjacent to the church. Surrounding the whole complex was a moat, though now largely infilled. Attached to the south side of the churchyard, within the tree-covered plot in the foreground is an exceptionally fine series of eight interconnected fishponds, most of them still partially water-filled.

At the Reformation in the sixteenth century the college was dissolved and the chapel became a parish church. During the eighteenth century the church fell into disrepair and was thoroughly restored in 1861-2. More recently it has been refurbished once again and is now vested in the Redundant Churches Fund.

Standing alone in tranquil surroundings the church is a splendid monument to a bloody event in our Nation's history.

Photo 82

WENLOCK PRIORY

An Anglo-Saxon monastery was founded at Wenlock about AD 680 by Merewalh, King of the Magonsaete. Shortly afterwards Merewalh's daughter Mildburg became its abbess, and her fame was to result in her later being canonised. After the death of St. Mildburg around AD 727 little is known of the monastery's history until the Norman Conquest. Some time between 1079 and 1082 Earl Roger de Montgomery refounded a monastic community at Wenlock as a Cluniac Priory. The Priory grew rapidly and during the first half of the fourteenth century the priory church was completely rebuilt on a lavish scale. It was a noble structure, one hundred and seven metres in length, with a nave of eight bays and a chancel of seven bays. Of this church, the impressive ruins of the north and south transept and the south end of the nave still survive, while the remainder of the church can clearly be seen in the surviving wall-footings. The rectangular cloister is also evident to the left of the church, with its octagonal 'lavatorium' or washing-place in its south-western corner. Next to the cloister can be seen a large L-shaped building, the infirmary and prior's lodge of about 1500, described as one of the finest examples of domestic architecture of this period in England. Following the dissolution of the Priory in 1540 these buildings were converted into a private residence and remain so to the present day.

By the mid-twelfth century a small town had developed under the shadow of the Priory; therein lies the origin of the Borough of Much Wenlock. Access from the town into the monastery precinct was originally through a gateway to the west of the Priory church. A tall square gatehouse tower of probable fourteenth century date still survives and can be seen to the left of the Priory flanking the access road to the Priory.

Photo 83

MEDIEVAL ABBEYS: HAUGHMOND AND BUILDWAS

The early history of Haughmond Abbey, near Shrewsbury, is obscure though its foundation certainly predates 1135 when an existing community there was richly endowed by William FitzAlan, Lord of Oswestry. Like most Augustinian foundations it was established in what was then a remote wooded area, and was to develop into one of the wealthiest and most prestigious monasteries in Shropshire.

The substantial and impressive ruins that survive today (Photograph 83) are largely confined to the conventual buildings (refectory, dormitories and the like), which at Haughmond are somewhat unusually based around a double cloister plan. Little survives of the church, though its excavated foundations allow its long nave, transepts and square-ended chancel to be seen at bottom left. Immediately right of the church is a square cloister, flanked on the

Photo 84

near side by the surviving inner wall of the west range and on the far side by the still-roofed chapter house, a magnificent construction of the twelfth century, though much altered in the sixteenth century. Further right again can be seen a second or outer cloister, flanked at far right by the most impressive surviving structures on this fascinating site – the thirteenth century abbot's lodging and an exceptionally fine fourteenth century hall.

Throughout its history Haughmond was one of the largest and most influential of Augustinian houses. To a large extent this depended on the benefactions of its founders and patrons, the FitzAlans, the greatest of all Shropshire landowners. The Abbey was dissolved in 1539, at which time there were still thirteen canons resident. After the Dissolution the Abbey buildings were converted by the Barker family into a fine mansion, accidentally burned down during the Civil War of 1642-6. Since 1949 the site has been in the care of the State, and every year it is visited by thousands of sightseers attracted both by the Abbey and by the fine wooded walks along the hillslopes to its east.

On the south bank of the River Severn, near the western end of the Ironbridge Gorge, lie the ruins of Buildwas Abbey (Photograph 84). Founded in 1135 it is the only house of the Cistercian order in Shropshire. Though never a particularly large or wealthy Abbey its

substantial remains today make it one of the finest surviving monastic sites in the Marches. An unusual feature of its plan is the location of the cloister on the *north* side of the church, to reflect the lie of the land here and to facilitate drainage towards the river. The Abbey is also remarkable in that its buildings were mostly completed by 1200 and remained almost unaltered until the Dissolution three and a half centuries later. Few monasteries display so little structural change and development.

The principal surviving building is the Abbey Church, cruciform in plan and measuring forty-nine metres in length. Like the rest of the buildings it displays a simplicity which reflects the ascetic ideals of the early Cistercian Order. Much of the Abbey's income was derived from wool, which during the thirteenth century was supplied to both Flemish and Italian merchants. Presumably most of this would have been shipped down the Severn, and for this Buildwas was admirably situated. The Abbey also supplemented its income by tolls levied on the adjacent bridge across the river. For most of its history Buildwas appears to have been well run and soundly managed, though on one occasion in 1342 the Abbot is said to have been murdered by one of the monks. Buildwas Abbey was finally dissolved in 1536 when Stephen Greene, the last Abbot, surrendered it to King Henry VIII.

Photo 85

Photo 86

SHREWSBURY

Standing proudly on a high ridge almost encircled by a meander of the Severn is the county town of Shrewsbury (Photograph 85). First recorded in AD 901 the town has continued as the administrative and commercial centre of Shropshire for over a thousand years. It was presumably the defensive potential offered by the loop of the River Severn that first attracted a fortified settlement here. By 1066

the town was sufficiently important and prosperous to have five churches, two hundred and fifty-two inhabited houses, and a royal mint. The nucleus of this early town probably lay on the ridge of high ground centred on the four ancient churches of St. Mary, St. Alkmund, St. Julian and St. Chad (top left to right in Photograph 85). After the Norman conquest Shrewsbury's strategic importance was

enhanced by the erection of a castle at the narrow neck of the river-loop, where it could control the landward approach to the town. The extensive and well-preserved remains of the castle are visible in the centre of Photograph 86 with the tree-covered sides of the tall motte towering above the river. To the left, and overlooked by the thirteenth century twin-towered Great Hall of the castle is the railway station, opened in 1848, and extending part way across the river on a seven-arched bridge.

By the thirteenth century Shrewsbury had become a large and wealthy town and in 1300 was accounted among the twelve richest in England, largely on the basis of its wool industry. This growth and prosperity resulted in a replanning of the town during the thirteenth century, including a new market place in the Square and a grid of streets off Mardol, Shoplatch and the south end of Pride Hill. The layout of this part of the town is splendidly illustrated in Photograph 87 with at its centre the sixteenth century Market Hall in the Square. In the foreground is the modern market hall and clock tower built in 1965 to replace a Victorian predecessor. Despite this and other large-scale modern redevelopments the town has retained much of its historic character. Picturesque sixteenth and seventeenth century timber-framed buildings grace streets and lanes which still follow their medieval pattern. Indeed, the timber-framed buildings, the steep winding streets and the narrow alleyways or 'shuts' are amongst Shrewsbury's abiding attractions, making it one of the most beautiful and interesting historic towns in England.

Photo 87

Photo 88

LUDLOW

Ludlow is the finest of Shropshire's planned medieval towns, and among the best preserved and most picturesque of England. Like many Shropshire towns it grew in the shadow of its medieval castle, founded during the late eleventh century by the Norman dynasty of the de Lacy's. The castle became one of the greatest fortresses of the Marches, and remains to this day one of the most impressive medieval castles in the kingdom. The original castle is the part now known as the inner bailey (the smaller walled area in the foreground of Photograph 88). It contains a remarkable circular Norman chapel and a magnificent fourteenth century hall and chamber blocks, while towering over the whole complex is a lofty twelfth century tower-keep. Late in the twelfth century the castle was effectively trebled in size by the addition of a large outer bailey.

During the earlier twelfth century a new town was laid out along the ridge on which the castle sits. A rectilinear grid-iron plan developed in a series of phases. The plan incorporated an earlier

Photo 89

Photo 90

north-south road, the present Old Street/Corve Street, running from right to left in the foreground of Photograph 89. Between this alignment and the castle extended High Street, a wide street that served as the principal market place, now considerably narrowed at its east by encroachment and infilling. The expanding town was provided with a church in 1199, of which fragments survive in the present St. Lawrence's. The church, cathedral-like in its proportions, is the largest and most impressive in Shropshire. It was substantially rebuilt in the fifteenth century on a lavish scale indicative of the town's prosperity during the later Middle Ages (Photograph 90). By the thirteenth century Ludlow had become a major centre of the wool and cloth industry, the third largest town in Shropshire. A town wall, 1.6 kilometres in circumference, was built between 1233 and 1304; extensive sections still survive and the wall has left its imprint on the topography of the town, truncating pre-existing burgage plots and streets. In 1475 Ludlow's importance was further enhanced when the castle became the seat of the Council of the Marches of Wales, which governed Wales and the border counties until 1689. In the eighteenth and nineteenth centuries the town became a fashionable social centre for the local gentry, a status still reflected in the wealth of Georgian houses that front its principal streets. Today Ludlow remains as it has been for the past eight hundred years, a thriving market town serving large parts of south Shropshire, and a tourist attraction for visitors from far and wide.

Photo 91

Photo 92

BRIDGNORTH

Few towns could rival Bridgnorth for beauty of setting, high on a sandstone ridge overlooking the River Severn in the south-eastern part of the county. From this vantage point the town has dominated the Severn Valley for almost nine hundred years. Throughout the Middle Ages the town's importance rested on its control of the river crossing at this point. A bridge had been built here by AD 896 and for centuries was to remain one of only two bridging points between Shrewbury and Worcester.

This strategic position prompted the construction of a 'burh' at *Bricge* in AD 912, by Aethelflaed of Mercia. This early settlement probably occupied the site of the later castle, on the jutting promontory that now forms the town park (top centre in Photograph 91). In 1101 this naturally defensive position was refortified by Robert de Belleme, as the site of his castle and borough of Bridgnorth. The castle was slighted by Parliament in 1646 but its fragmentary Norman keep (top centre) has survived as one of the most notable ruins in the county.

Next to the keep is St. Mary Magdalene's church, built in 1792 by Thomas Telford to replace the castle's medieval chapel. The early medieval borough was contained within the outer bailey of the castle, its layout has been fossilised in the horseshoe shape of East and West Castle Street (middleground). A later twelfth century development appears to have been the laying out of a typical long and wide High Street (foreground), with a series of narrower streets running off it at right angles. The Town Hall, which stands in the middle of the High Street, was built in 1648-52, after much of the town had been burned down during the Civil War in 1646. By 1300 Bridgnorth was the second most important town in Shropshire, its prosperity largely dependent on the river traffic and the bridge crossing. It remained a major river port until the opening of the Severn Valley Railway in 1862. Today the railway, whose station can be seen at top right (Photograph 91), is one of the few surviving steam-operated lines in Britain. Immediately beyond the station are the earthworks of the early medieval castle site known as Panpudding Hill.

The second of the two medieval churches in the historic core of Bridgnorth is that of St. Leonard's (photograph 92). This massive church is almost entirely Victorian, built in 1861-1862 to replace its medieval predecessor. It sits within a large circular churchyard; now surrounded by buildings, this is as prominent a feature of the townscape today as it was when it formed a distinct precinct within the plan of the medieval town. The northern course of Bridgnorth's medieval town wall lies in the immediate foreground, with the medieval North Gate, heavily restored in 1910, visible at the bottom right.

Photo 93

NEWPORT

The very name Newport illustrates the town's origin as a planned foundation of the Middle Ages, established during the reign of Henry I (1100-1135), who visited the town twice. After almost nine hundred years the medieval plan is still visible from the air. Essentially it consists of a long, wide and winding High Street, with narrow regular burgage plots (holdings), leading off from either side at right angles. In the centre of the town is the parish church of St. Nicholas, largely rebuilt in the nineteenth century, though the tower is fourteenth century in date. Its central position betrays its foundation as part of the medieval borough, although it did not gain full parochial status until 1221. The church and churchyard stand on an 'island' where High Street broadens out

to accommodate the borough's original market place, now replaced by the triangular 'wedge' of buildings beyond the church. Few buildings in Newport predate the seventeenth century, a great fire in 1665 having destroyed much of the town.

When founded in the early twelfth century the town stood within an area of meres and marshland forming part of the royal manor of Edgmond. One of these meres, along the north side of the town, was an important fishery. The economic origins of the town are neatly illustrated by its obligation to carry fish to the royal court, and to this day the town's coat of arms comprises three fishes.

OSWESTRY

Photo 94

The town of Oswestry in north-west Shropshire grew up during the twelfth century in the shadow of a castle founded about 1086 by Rainald, Sheriff of Shropshire. It was carved out of the Anglo-Saxon manor of Maesbury, which it soon displaced in importance; by 1114 it had become head of the FitzAlan lordship which bore its name. The Norman castle still survives as a large tree-covered mound in the centre of the town (top left in this aerial view from the south). A large bailey extended to the right of the motte and within this was sited the early nucleus of the town. By 1276 twenty-two burgage plots had been laid out within the bailey and market stalls were erected there between 1327 and 1330. To this day the weekly market is still held in the open area known as Bailey Head adjacent to the castle mound. The town was granted its borough charter in 1198 and developed in a 'horseshoe' shape, the three main streets, Willow, Leg and Beatrice Street being laid out to skirt the castle defences.

The impressive square-towered parish church of St. Oswald, in the foreground, is curiously located some three hundred metres south of the historic core of the town. It already existed by 1085 and may mark the nucleus of an earlier settlement, predating the medieval castle and town. Both the church and the facing Church Street formed part of an extra-mural suburb created when the central areas of Oswestry were provided with a town wall between 1257 and 1304. The suburb was known as *Chirton*, and in it resided Oswestry's wealthier burgesses. Despite frequent Welsh attacks the town continued to flourish and by the sixteenth century had become the principal market centre for Welsh cloth, a trend that began in the Middle Ages. Today, Oswestry remains an important regional centre, thronged by visitors from the surrounding countryside on Wednesday market days.

BISHOPS CASTLE

Bishops Castle is a medieval plantation that owes both its origin and its name to the Bishops of Hereford, who founded a castle here some time in the early twelfth century. The castle was sited on a naturally defensive spur within the bishops' great estate of Lydbury North. A town had been established by the end of the century on the steep south-facing slope below the castle, creating a single unit of strategic and economic importance. This view shows the castle in the foreground, with its inner bailey now used as a bowling green, and the course of its outer bailey marked by the curving roads that surround it. Beyond this stretches the town, laid out on a rectilinear grid, with narrow burgage plots on either side of a long and steeply sloping High Street. The medieval market place, now largely built-over, stood at the top of the High Street at its junction with the outer bailey of the castle. At the far end of the town the parish church of St. John the Baptist, first mentioned in 1291, stands within a large churchyard. Its peripheral location hints at a late addition to the town plan though its foundation must have occurred before the end of the twelfth century; its massive squat tower is clearly Norman in date. The town never developed into a flourishing commercial centre and despite being granted a market charter in 1248 it did not gain borough status until 1573. Even today Bishops Castle has hardly grown beyond the confines of the medieval town. In 1961 it had the smallest recorded population of any English borough, finally losing its municipal status in 1966.

Photo 95

Photo 96

MARKET DRAYTON

The north Shropshire town of Market Drayton originated during the mid-thirteenth century, when Combermere Abbey (in Cheshire) developed an existing village site into a planned town. Following the granting of a market charter in 1245 the town successfully expanded into a local market centre, a role it fulfils to the present day. The long and wide High Street, and the parallel curving Cheshire Street form the central elements of the town plan; both were laid out in the Middle Ages. At the head of High Street stands the parish church of St. Mary dramatically sited at the top of a steep hill overlooking the River Tern. The church has occupied this site since at least the twelfth century, its tall fourteenth century tower still dominates the town. A disastrous fire in 1651 destroyed much of the town centre and few buildings earlier than this survive within the historic core. The opening of the Birmingham and Liverpool Junction Canal through Market Drayton in 1835 ensured the continuing prosperity of the town, which remains to this day a popular port of call to travellers along the inland waterways.

Photo 97

ATTINGHAM HALL AND PARK

Attingham is probably the finest house of its period in Shropshire, and certainly the best known. It lies next to the village of Atcham, near the confluence of the Rivers Tern and Severn, some eight kilometres south-east of Shrewsbury. The Hall was built for the first Lord Berwick in 1783-5, to the design of George Stuart, incorporating parts of an earlier eighteenth century house called Tern Hall. Interior alterations were made by John Nash in 1807-10. The view shows the Hall from the rear, with its attached courtyard and impressive quadrangular stable block in the foreground. The Hall itself is a magnificent ashlar-faced edifice, eleven bays wide and two and a half storeys high, with projecting colonnades connecting it to low service wings on either side.

The great landscape designer Humphrey Repton was employed to improve the surrounding park in 1789, and much of his landscape survives to the present day. Repton made great play of the River Tern, which cuts through the middle of the estate (just beyond the Hall in this view). Large expanses of water were created along the course of the Tern, perhaps partially re-using the ponds of an ironworks that operated here until 1757.

Since 1953 the house and the park have been in the care of the National Trust, the magnificence of the Hall and the beauty of its landscaped Park drawing visitors from all parts of Britain.

Photo 98

Photo 99

HAWKSTONE PARK

Set among a series of dramatic sandstone cliffs and ridges that rise above the north Shropshire Plain is the landscaped estate of Hawkstone Park. During the eighteenth century this naturally scenic area was improved and developed into one of the most picturesque and spectacular man-made landscapes in England. At its heart lies Hawkstone Hall (Photograph 98) built in about 1720 for Sir Richard Hill, the wings being added about thirty years later for his nephew Sir Rowland Hill. Behind the house extends the ornamental Temple Walk, in existence by 1784 and named after the two-domed rotundas disposed along it. Today the house is a religious college; hence the church, built in 1934 that lies immediately to its right. Fine building that it is, Hawkstone Hall is nevertheless surpassed by the splendour of the surrounding park, created by successive generations of the Hill family from about 1740 onwards. Terraced walks, caves, arbours, grottoes and follies were linked together to create a series of 'experiences' and views. Typical of these is Grotto Hill (Photograph 99) on a projecting sandstone cliff from which there are breathtaking vistas across north Shropshire, Cheshire and the foothills of North Wales. Here, on the summit of the cliff, existing caves were enlarged to create galleries supported by free-standing columns. A small chamber, partly cut out of the rock but mostly constructed in rubble stonework, originally had internal ceilings and walls which were decorated with shells and coloured stones. Above this chamber was an artificial ruin, still intact, comprising an incomplete gothic stonework arch. This remarkable structure epitomises the spirit of Hawkstone: picturesque, romantic and dramatic, a stunning realisation of the late eighteenth century concept of the sublime as embodied in the natural landscape.

Photo 100

ALDENHAM PARK

The creation of landscaped parks has had a major impact on the Shropshire countryside over the past three hundred years. Even where parks no longer survive in their original form and extent, their imprint on the landscape can still be dramatic, as at Aldenham Park near Morville, five kilometres north-west of Bridgnorth. A landscaped park of a hundred hectares was created here during the seventeenth century. In 1691 the house at its centre was rebuilt for Sir Edward Acton and soon afterwards the existing park was redesigned on an even grander scale. Most of the park has since been enclosed for farming purposes, except for a small area immediately around the house. Strikingly intact, however, is a magnificent avenue leading to the house itself. Over a thousand metres in length and lined with mature lime-trees this is still a most impressive landscape feature. It had been laid out by 1722, its entrance onto what is now the main A442 road being screened by a splendid pair of wrought iron gates made in 1718. The sheer length and directness of this drive contrasts starkly with the modest scale of the house itself, and with the wide-spreading informality of the park in its original form; presumably this was a deliberate, if rather eccentric, device to enhance the impact of both.

Photo 101

COALBROOKDALE

Within Coalbrookdale, a steep-sided valley running north from the Ironbridge Gorge, were conceived industrial innovations that became the catalyst for the industrial revolution. The large modern foundry in the Dale is only the latest in a succession of ironworks that have existed here since at least the sixteenth century. The most crucial development, however, occurred in 1709 when Abraham Darby first smelted iron ore with the aid of coke instead of charcoal. The 'Old Furnace' used for this breakthrough still stands beneath a tent-like cover building at top right in this view. In subsequent years the Darbys enlarged the ironworks of their Coalbrookdale Company; among many innovative achievements was the casting of the magnificent iron trusses for the nearby Ironbridge (Photograph l02). In the middleground stands the Great Warehouse, built in 1838, with an ornate clock tower added in 1843. The building was restored in the 1970s for use as a museum of iron. A railway line connecting Coalbrookdale to the main-line routes and other centres was opened in 1864, the imposing curve of its brick viaduct still dominating the valley.

Overlooking the ironworks are many eighteenth and nineteenth century houses, formerly the homes of ironmasters and their workforce. Among them is Dale House, the tall red brick building at top centre, built by Abraham Darby I in 1715 and occupied by successive ironmasters and managers of the Coalbrookdale Works. The completeness of this industrial landscape of works, houses and communication systems has resulted in the area's designation as a World Heritage Site.

THE IRONBRIDGE GORGE

For a period of about forty years at the end of the eighteenth century the Ironbridge Gorge was the most important ironworking centre in Britain.   Within this wooded district of the East Shropshire Coalfield were pioneered many of the innovations in the manufacture and use of iron that were to fuel the Industrial Revolution.   The best known and in many ways the most symbolic monument of this period of industrial pre-eminence is the iron bridge that spans the River Severn, and which gives the area its name. This elegant structure, built in 1777-1781 by Abraham Darby III was the world's first cast-iron bridge and also the first successful large-scale structural   use of cast iron.   The bridge became the focus for a small commercial centre based round an open market-square at the north (left-hand) end of the bridge. This was laid out in the 1780s and is one of the few elements of formal planning in the Ironbridge Gorge.

On the steep hillside above the market place a network of narrow paths and lanes links an informal layout of buildings ranging from cottages of the seventeenth and early eighteenth centuries to large and imposing Victorian villas.   Many of these fairways originated as packhorse tracks and primitive railways serving numerous coal mines along the sides of the Gorge.   Following a long period of stagnation and decline from about the 1890s the area has more recently become a centre of renewed commercial activity in the new town of Telford. It has also developed as a tourist attraction of international renown, with many of its buildings restored as museums of the Industrial Revolution.

Photo 102

Photo 103

SNAILBEACH LEAD MINE

The lead field of south-west Shropshire was once one of the most productive and important lead mining regions in Britain. At its heart lay Snailbeach, three kilometres south of Minsterley, the biggest and richest of all the Shropshire mines. Although mining may have taken place here from the Roman period the first historical reference dates from 1676. In 1783 the Snailbeach Mining Company was formed and by the second half of the nineteenth century the mine was one of the foremost national producers of lead perhaps even the richest mine in Europe. Barytes was mined from 1860, becoming the main ore extracted from 1910 onwards. The twentieth century has seen a gradual contraction of operations, and underground working finally ceased in 1955. Abundant above-ground remains survive to testify to the former industrial importance of the site. The most vivid is the White Tip a huge heap of waste spar from the processing of lead ore. Most of this material was deposited between 1835 and 1864, its toxic nature keeping it free of plant-growth, a stark and prominent feature dominating the landscape. Extensive structural remains of the mine also survive. These include the tall Lordshill chimney, visible in the foreground, built in 1885 to serve the mine's smeltworks. Within the wooded area beyond can be made out the ruins of a nineteenth century engine-house. Altogether, the well-preserved mining remains at Snailbeach are spread over an area of half a square kilometre, making this one of the most important industrial archaeology sites in the region.

CLEE HILL INDUSTRIAL REMAINS

The Clee Hills of South Shropshire contain a wealth of minerals that have been exploited for centuries to create one of the most remarkable industrial landscapes in the region. Coal, ironstone, limestone and basalt are all found here and as early as 1235 coal was being taken from Titterstone Clee. John Leland in the sixteenth century refers to *"a blo shope on Titterstone Clee"*, probably a wind furnace for the smelting of iron ore. By 1727 coal from Titterstone Clee was valued at £1500 per year.

The result of this past industrial activity is strikingly evident in this bird's eye view of the lower slopes of Clee Hill, near Doddington. The circular mounds consist of spoil from underground workings, heaped around the mouths of shallow mine shafts (bell-pits). After abandonment the shafts have collapsed, leaving a characteristic hollow at the centre of each mound. Most of these bell-pit mines were for the extraction of coal, although ironstone was also worked in this way. This method of mining was in operation from the Middle Ages to the seventeenth century. The mines seen here could date from any time during this period, probably representing piecemeal mining over a considerable length of time. They owe their excellent state of preservation to the area's status as common grazing land. Only in peripheral areas have the mining remains been removed, as at Doddington itself, where squatter settlements (on the left of the photograph) have encroached into the former mining areas. But even here the bell-pit mines can still be made out as low, gently-rounded mounds in the green grassy paddocks.

Photo 104

Photo 105

TITTERSTONE CLEE

The dramatic and distinctive outline of Titterstone Clee is one of the most familiar landmarks of the south Shropshire skyline, its outline enhanced in recent years by the gleaming white radar domes on its summit. In prehistoric times the hilltop was occupied by the largest hillfort in Shropshire, enclosing twenty-eight hectares. Its ruined stone rampart can be seen here, curving round the right side of the hill, though much of its course has been destroyed by the huge stone quarries gouged into the western side of the hill from the nineteenth century onwards. The basalt rock which caps the hilltop, known locally as Dhustone, was the impetus for this quarrying. The quarries were opened in 1881 at a time when the Clee Hills were the centre of a major quarrying industry, with as many as two thousand people employed. Huge quantities of the local rock, used mainly as roadstone, were transported from the hilltop quarry by means of an inclined plane to Bitterley village almost two hundred and fifty metres below and one and a half kilometres distant. In the foreground, on the lower slopes of the hill, can be seen the bell-pit mounds of earlier industrial activity. Quarrying on Titterstone Clee finally ceased in the 1980s but extractive industries have left a striking and permanent imprint on the landscape.

LLANYMYNECH

The mineral wealth of Llanymynech Hill, on the Shropshire/Wales border, has been exploited for centuries. Copper and lead are both likely to have been mined here in prehistoric and Roman times, and the summit of the hill is surrounded by the ramparts of one of the largest of all known hillforts. But it is the quarrying and processing of lime that has had the most dramatic impact on the area's landscape. The foreground of Photograph 106 shows the heavily quarried south side of the hill, where a series of quarries have been cut and recut until all open into a single large quarry. This quarrying activity was at its most intense during the eighteenth and nineteenth centuries, although it continued well into this century. After quarrying the limestone was moved down the steep hillside via two inclined planes which led to a series of lime-burning kilns on the lower ground to the south. From here the lime was transported along the adjacent Ellesmere Canal that was opened in 1796. The curving course of the canal is visible beyond the wooded area in the middle distance.

Rising above the trees is the tall brick chimney of an unusual Hoffmann type kiln built c. 1900 for the firing of lime. This kiln still survives largely intact and can be seen in detail in Photograph l07. Between it and the canal runs the straight tree-lined route of the railway, built in 1860, which effectively superseded the canal as the principal means of transport for the Llanymynech limestone industry.

Photo 106

110

Photo 107

Photo 108

CHIRK VIADUCTS

Off-setting one another in the valley of the River Ceiriog, on the north Shropshire border with Wales at Chirk, stand a canal aqueduct and a railway viaduct. Each is a magnificent engineering and architectural achievement in its own right. Together they present a spectacle of stunning impact, both from the ground and from the air.

The earlier of the two is the aqueduct, designed by Thomas Telford to carry the Ellesmere Canal and completed in 1801. It is one hundred and eighty-three metres in length and stands twenty-one metres high on ten masonry arches with hollow piers carried up between them like pilaster strips. The canal itself is carried on a bed of cast-iron plates, with side walls built up of stone. The aqueduct took five years to build, at a cost of nearly twenty-one thousand pounds and for a time it was the longest in the country. Still in operation today, it is one of the most spectacular structures of England's inland waterways. Dominating Telford's aqueduct is the higher and longer railway viaduct, built in 1846-8 to carry the Shrewsbury-Chester railway line. This magnificent sixteen-arched structure, two hundred and fifty-nine metres in length, stands over thirty metres high above the valley floor. Initially, the three arches at either end were built of specially laminated wood, to speed up the opening of the line, though they were rebuilt in stone in 1858-9. Like the aqueduct this fine structure is still in use today, its purpose and effectiveness unchanged a century and a half after its original construction.

Photo 109

CRAVEN ARMS

Craven Arms stands at the convergence of a number of ancient valley and ridge-top routes. At such a naturally important position one would expect an early settlement, yet the town is entirely a creation of the second half of the nineteenth century. Until the coming of the railways the site accommodated little more than an inn near the hamlet of Newtown in the parish of Stokesay. First the Shrewsbury-Hereford line, in 1852, then the Knighton line to mid-Wales, in 1861, turned Craven Arms into an important railway junction. The Earl of Craven sought to exploit this by creating a new town, laid out as a rectangular grid of streets with regular property plots. The growth of an important livestock market soon established the economic survival of the town. This view shows Craven Arms from the south, with the Shrewsbury-Hereford railway line running straight through it. The original planned nucleus lies to the right of the railway, between the main A49 road and the curving course of the River Onny (far right); the areas left of the railway are mostly twentieth century expansion. The original Craven Arms Inn, a large brick building of about 1825, still stands between the railway and the A49 road, opposite the open livestock market. In the distance, running from right to left and by-passing Craven Arms, is the Roman road from Wroxeter to Leintwardine, emphasising that for centuries before the coming of the railways the Craven Arms gap was an important communication corridor.

LIST OF AERIAL PHOTOGRAPHS

For each photograph the place name is given together with the negative number and the date of photography.

CPAT = Clwyd-Powys Archaeological Trust.
CUCAP = Cambridge University Committee for Aerial Photography.

1. Linley Hill Earthworks
    (CPAT 87-C-29, 3rd January 1987)
2. Castle Idris (CPAT 86-MB-214, 25th February 1986)
3. Bwlch Farm Enclosure
    (CPAT 84-11-14, 24th April 1984)
4. Cropmark Enclosure near Adcote
    (CPAT 86-MB-764, 19th July 1986)
5. Rowley Enclosure (CPAT 83-20-2, 13th August 1983)
6. Stocktonwood Hillfort (CPAT 90-C-374, 31 July 1990)
7. Boreatton Hall (CPAT 90-MB-790, 28th June 1990)
8. Whixall Moss (CPAT 84-23-9A, 26th June 1984)
9. North Shropshire Lakes
    (CPAT 92-C-1064, 19th July 1992)
10. The River Severn (CPAT 92-C-1044, 19th July 1992)
11. Wenlock Edge (CUCAP WQ-80, 1956)
12. Wyre Forest (CPAT 92-MC15-16, 15th May 1992)
13. The Long Mynd (CPAT 93-MC02-06, 21st May1993)
14. Norton Farm Quarry, Condover
    (CPAT 90-C-106, 19th June 1990)
15. The Roveries, Lydham (CPAT 85-16-2, 23rd July 1985)
16. Prehistoric Ritual Sites at Strefford
    (CUCAP BUL-92, July 1975)
17. Round Hill Barrow near Pennerley
    (CPAT 88-MB-473, 30th October 1988)
18. Stiperstones Cairn (CPAT 93-C-586, 21st May 1993)
19. Baschurch Ring-Ditches
    (CPAT 86-MB-771, 19th July 1986)
20. Baschurch Ring-Ditch
    (CPAT 90-MB-788, 29th June 1990)
21. Mitchell's Fold Stone Circle
    (CPAT 93-MC02-15, 21st May 1993)
22. Hoarstone Stone Circle
    (CPAT 92-MB-417, 3rd May 1992)
23. Long Mynd Field System
    (CPAT 84-C-478, 11th December 1984)
24. Stapeley Hill Field System
    (CPAT 83-C-588, 23 November 1983)
25. Caer Din Ring (CPAT 85-C-254, 23rd July 1985)
26. Stitt Hill Enclosure and Dykes
    (CPAT 87-C-34, 3rd January 1987)
27. Caer Caradoc Hillfort, Chapel Lawn
    (CPAT 87-C-4 3rd January 1987)
28. Bury Ditches (CPAT 89-C-224, 11th July 1989)
29. Burrow Hill Camp (CPAT 90-C-366, 31st July 1990)
30. Nordy Bank Hillfort
    (CPAT 89-MB-98, 20th February 1989)
31. Old Oswestry (CPAT 92-MB-752, 19th July 1992)
32. Old Oswestry (CPAT 93-MB-86, 1st January 1993)
33. The Berth (CPAT 84-MB-176, 15th July 1984)
34. Crickheath Wharf Enclosure
    (CPAT 84-24-37, 26th June 1984)
35. Culmington Enclosures
    (CPAT 90-C-208, 13th July 1990)
36. Shelvock Enclosures (CPAT 90-C-323, 20th July 1990)
37. Osbaston Enclosure (CPAT 84-MB-253, 19th July 1984)
38. Berghill Enclosures (CPAT 90-MB-797, 28th June 1990)
39. Roman Fort at Wroxeter (CUCAP TN-39, 1956)
40. Rhyn Park (CPAT 84-C-236, 19th July 1984)
41. Wall Town Fort (CPAT 92-MC18-8, 26th June 1992)
42. Roman Marching Camp at Bromfield
    (CUCAP BYS-39, July 1976)
43. Whitchurch (CPAT 92-C-758, 5th May 1992)
44. Linley Hill Earthwork (CPAT 85-C-79, 12th March 1985)
45. Edenhope Hill Enclosure
    (CPAT 84-C-10, 30th March 1984)
46. Watling Street Roman Road (CUCAP Y-84, July 1947)
47. Wroxeter Roman Town (CUCAP RC8 BC04, July 1975)
48. Wroxeter Roman Town
    (CPAT 93-MB-46, 1st January 1993)

SUGGESTED FURTHER READING

Millward, R. & Robinson, A., — The Welsh Borders, (Eyre Methuen, 1978)

Pevsner, N., — The Buildings of England: Shropshire, (Penguin, 1958)

Rowley, T., — The Shropshire Landscape, (Hodder & Stoughton, 1972)

Rowley, T., — The Landscape of the Welsh Marches, (Michael Joseph, 1986)

Stamper, P., — The Farmer Feeds Us All, (Shropshire Books, 1989)

Stanford, S.C., — The Archaeology of the Welsh Marches, 2nd.ed. (S.C.Stanford, 1991)

Toghill, P., — Geology in Shrophire, (Swan Hill Press, 1990)

Trinder, B., — The Industrial Revolution in Shropshire, (Phillimore, 1973)

Trinder, B., — History of Shropshire, (Phillimore, 1983)

Webster, G., — The Cornovii, 2nd. ed., (Alan Sutton, 1991)

Whimster, R., — The Emerging Past: Air Photography and the Buried Landscape, (RCHME, 1989)

Wilson, D.R., — Air Photo Interpretation for Archaeologists, (Batsford, 1982)

More books on Shropshire's landscape
and history published by Shropshire Books

THE FARMER FEEDS US ALL	Paul Stamper	£4.95
CASTLES OF SHROPSHIRE	Michael Jackson	£5.95
MONASTIC SHROPSHIRE	G.C.Baugh	£2.50
SHROPSHIRE COUNTY GUIDE		£3.50

Forthcoming title:

SHROPSHIRE SEASONS

Gordon Dickins

Spectacular full-colour photographs
of Shropshire through the seasons
by renowned photographer and expert
on the county, Gordon Dickins.

For a complete list of Shropshire Books titles, please contact:

Shropshire Books,
Shropshire County Council,
Leisure Services Department,
Winston Churchill Building,
Radbrook Centre,
SHREWSBURY, SY3 9BJ.
Telephone: (0743) 254043